GAMES, SPORT AND POWER

transaction book series

TA-1 *Campus Power Struggle*/Howard S. Becker

TA-2 *Cuban Communism*/Irving Louis Horowitz

TA-3 *The Changing South*/Raymond W. Mack

TA-4 *Where Medicine Fails*/Anselm L. Strauss

TA-5 *The Sexual Scene*/John H. Gagnon and William Simon

TA-6 *Black Experience: Soul*/Lee Rainwater

TA-7 *Black Experience: The Transformation of Activism*/August Meier

TA-8 *Law and Order: Modern Criminals*/James F. Short, Jr.

TA-9 *Law and Order: The Scales of Justice*/Abraham S. Blumberg

TA-10 *Social Science and National Policy*/Fred R. Harris

TA-11 *Peace and the War Industry*/Kenneth E. Boulding

TA-12 *America and the Asian Revolutions*/Robert Jay Lifton

TA-13 *Law and Order: Police Encounters*/Michael Lipsky

TA-14 *American Bureaucracy*/Warren G. Bennis

TA-15 *The Values of Social Science*/Norman K. Denzin

TA-16 *Ghetto Revolts*/Peter H. Rossi

TA-17 *The Future Society*/Donald N. Michael

TA-18 *Awakening Minorities: American Indians, Mexican Americans, Puerto Ricans*/John R. Howard

TA-19 *The American Military*/Martin Oppenheimer

TA-20 *Total Institutions*/Samuel E. Wallace

TA-21 *The Anti-American Generation*/Edgar Z. Friedenberg

TA-22 *Religion in Radical Transition*/Jeffrey K. Hadden

TA-23 *Culture and Civility in San Francisco*/Howard S. Becker

TA-24 *Poor Americans: How the White Poor Live*/Marc Pilisuk and Phyllis Pilisuk

TA-25 *Games, Sport and Power*/Gregory P. Stone

GAMES, SPORT AND POWER

Edited by
GREGORY P. STONE

*trans*action *books*
New Brunswick, New Jersey
Distributed by E. P. Dutton and Company

Unless otherwise indicated, the essays in this book originally appeared in *trans*action magazine

*trans*action *books*
Rutgers University
New Brunswick, New Jersey 08903

Library of Congress Catalog Card Number: 78-164977
ISBN: 0-87855-003-8 (cloth); 0-87855-503-X (paper)

Printed in the United States of America

Contents

Preface   vii

Introduction
    Gregory P. Stone   1

Part One: GAMES

Of Pool Playing and Poolrooms
    Ned Polsky   19

Why People Play Poker
    Thomas M. Martinez and Robert La Franchi   55

Making *vs.* Playing Games of Cards
    E. Louis Mahigel and Gregory P. Stone   74

Part Two: SPORT

Athletes Are Not Inferior Students
    Walter E. Schafer and J. Michael Armer   97

The Affluent Baseball Player
    Ralph Andreano   117

Magic in Professional Baseball
    George Gmelch   128

Soccer as a Brazilian Way of Life
    Janet Lever   138

Part Three: THE CONTROL OF PLAY VERSUS PLAY AS CONTROL

Classical Music and the Status Game
    Joseph Bensman   163

Audiences—and All That Jazz
    Richard A. Peterson   178

The Dance Studio—Style Without Sex
    Helena Znaniecki Lopata
    and Joseph R. Noel   184

The Private Lives of Public Museums
    César Graña   202

Authority in the Comics
    Arthur A. Berger   217

Notes on Contributors   229

Preface

For the past eight years, *trans*action magazine has dedicated itself to the task of reporting the strains and conflicts within the American system. But the magazine has done more than this. It has pioneered in social programs for changing the society, offered the kind of analysis that has permanently restructured the terms of the "dialogue" between peoples and publics, and offered the sort of prognosis that makes for real alterations in social and political policies directly affecting our lives.

The work done in the pages of *trans*action has crossed disciplinary boundaries. This represents much more than simple cross-disciplinary "team efforts." It embodies rather a recognition that the social world cannot be easily carved into neat academic disciplines; that, indeed, the study of the experience of blacks in American ghettos, or the manifold uses and abuses of agencies of law enforcement, or the sorts of overseas policies that lead to the celebration of some dictatorships and the condemnation of others, can best be examined from many viewpoints and from the vantage points of many disciplines.

Now the editors of *trans*action magazine are making available in permanent form the most important work done in the magazine, supplemented in some cases by additional materials edited to reflect the tone and style developed over the years by *trans*action. Like the magazine, this series of books demonstrates the superiority of starting with real world problems and searching out practical solutions, over the zealous guardianship of professional boundaries. Indeed, it is precisely this approach that has elicited enthusiastic support from leading American social scientists, many of whom are represented among the editors of these volumes.

The subject matter of these books concerns social changes and social policies that have aroused the long-standing needs and present-day anxieties of us all. These changes are in organizational lifestyles, concepts of human ability and intelligence, changing patterns of norms and morals, the relationship of social conditions to physical and biological environments, and in the status of social science with respect to national policy making. The editors feel that many of these articles have withstood the test of time, and match in durable interest the best of available social science literature. This collection of *trans*action articles, then, attempts to address itself to immediate issues without violating the basic insights derived from the classical literature in the various fields of social science.

As the crises of the sixties have given way to the economic crunch of the seventies, the social scientists involved as editors and authors of this series have gone beyond observation of critical areas, and have entered into the vital and difficult tasks of explanation and interpretation. They have defined issues in a way that makes solutions possible. They have provided answers as well as asked the right questions. These books, based as they are upon the best materials from *trans*action magazine, are dedicated not to the highlighting of social problems alone, but to establishing guidelines for social solutions based on the social sciences.

THE EDITORS
*trans*action

Introduction

GREGORY P. STONE

In a now classic *tour de force,* Huizinga labelled man *homo ludens*—man, the player. Indeed, men play, as do women, and even children, but the notion of play remains ambiguous, as Susanna Miller has pointed out so well in her recent *The Psychology of Play*. It is one of those concepts that Wittgenstein might have said has been wrapped in so much toilet paper that it looks round. The cutting edges and corners have been dulled, blunted or cushioned. The concept rolls rather than rocks or teeters. This book maintains the roll. Those vulnerable to *mal de mer* or vertigo would do well to reach for dramamine before turning its pages.

Here, we mine the drama provided by those astute unravellers of tangled toilet paper whose articles have appeared in *trans*action. Alexander was never so playful. He simply cut the Gordian tangle. Nor should sociologists take offense at my use of the dramatic metaphor.

1

After all, the best a social scientist can do is to dramatize his era so that others take it into account, as Marx, Veblen and Freud dramatized the life and organization of Western industrial society, and as Galbraith, Riesman, and McLuhan or perhaps Reich are dramatizing that era Rostow calls the "stage of high mass consumption." Then, of course, the laity, taking these dramatizations into account, alter their conduct. This poses new problems, and new dramatists emerge.

Why do we know so much and, consequently, so very little about play? Quite probably *because* the word has been wrapped with so much toilet paper. Or, like a snowball, the word has become incomprehensibly huge as it has been pushed and rolled over that vast snowfield of meaning which blankets historical time. Play—good grief! We think of amusement, being amused, drama (the play's the thing!), plays on words, playing a musical instrument, playing a game, a play in a game, foul play, the play of a belt or chain that drives a machine, pardonable pretense or jest, playboys, playmates, playing at the games people play and, of course, sport. Neither do these begin to exhaust the meanings that have been packed onto *that* snowball, nor is the problem of play merely the compounding and elaboration of meaning. The simple mention of sport establishes the fact that play has become infected with its conventionally accepted contrast—work—for sport is working at play. Yet, we can observe that sport occurs when nonplayers take time out from work to watch it!

In the world of sport, one works hard (like actors or players) to amuse onlookers or (like industrialists) to break records so that one might test (as Harry Stack Sullivan would have it) the reflected appraisals of others—one's parents, one's peers, one's coach, the "house" or one's nation, not to speak of oneself. So, there is the business of it all. Enjoyment gets sucked into work. This we can endure. What lies at the basis of much current shame and confusion in the United States, it seems to me, is that work is sucked into enjoyment. We hide our pleasure at work, pay heavily for our work at pleasure, and we live *la dolce vita*.

In an age of high mass consumption we are haunted by the ghosts of work, the ghosts of the nineteenth century. Perhaps Henry Ford, as David Riesman has suggested, or John Foster Dulles—each born after his time—have become ghosts who remind us of the end of an era. Sociologists, too, are haunted by such Protestant (and Marxist!) ectoplasm. Ghosts are history's patrolmen, and those who no longer control and patrol old vacant houses, castles or graveyards seem to patrol routes of transportation—roads, foot paths and bridges. We can generalize routes of transportation to include routes of communication, and particularize those by focusing on journals of sociology. These are often patrolled by ghosts.

When sociologists speak of play, those ghosts who control and patrol the journals strike terror into their hearts! In the not too distant past, a colleague and good friend submitted an article on camping (the outdoorsy type) to the *American Sociological Review*. It was turned down by the ghost in charge (known as the editor) with the harsh admonition that the article might better be published in *Outdoor Life* or *Sports Afield*. These, then, were looked upon as profane burying places, not being as sacred as such graveyards as the *American Sociological Review*. Of course, that editor did not relegate works on work to chamber of commerce publications, nor those having to do with industrial relations or management to trade or industrial union periodicals. Sociological works on work are not as often consigned to some profane potter's field. So it took that sometime savior of sociological sensibility, the *American Journal of Sociology,* to find an ultimate resting place for my good friend's article. Even so, it is very difficult to find a resting place for an article on play in the graveyards staked out by major journals of sociology. Consult the gravestones—I mean, of course, the tables of contents!

In contrast, *trans*action has provided a resting place for speculation, theory and research on play that has been denied by other sectarian keepers of communicative soil and resting places. In selecting articles for this volume, I could choose among a number of qualified applicants for resurrection from the cold journalistic earth into the heaven of a book considerably exceeding the number of such articles interred in the major journals. Perhaps unintentionally, but nevertheless sensitively, *trans*action has responded to a plea made more than 15 years ago by Nelson Foote, who professed his "deadly seriousness" about the necessity for a sociology of play. The other journals have not responded, patrolled as they are by the ghosts of work.

In attempting to bring together the articles presented in the following pages, I listed a number of terms, hoping they would generate a set of organizing categories—play, entertainment, games, drama, sport *and work.* But these terms all move together into one another and break apart all at once. The effort failed. George Herbert Mead confused play with drama in his speculation about the play of little children—playing house, school, store, and cowboys and Indians, or cops and robbers. Both play and drama are entertaining. But what is entertainment? Entertainment is established by surprise. Someone at a staid cocktail party comes up with a new unheard-of joke or a spontaneous *bon mot.* Others express a relieved laughter. It occurs in play as in tickling or mocking children (then the mocker is entertained, but the mocked is not, and the tickled one is on the edge of pain). Games may be vivacious—lively. They are played, but players must work at them, and such work may carry with it the peril of death, for example, the "contract" for the incompetent cheater who gambles in the United States. Living the game may also mean the early death of the player—the jai alai player in Latin America. One may work oneself to death to achieve eminence in the game—or in the play. The professional wrestler, a superb dramatist, fears most of all the failure of the heart.

Achieving eminence—stardom—who is to say that the star is not an actor, a performer? Is the baseball player who makes a difficult catch with the expressive simplicity of one hand an actor, or has he escaped the role by developing a style? The terms blend and merge in an unanalyzable amalgam.

I surrendered and decided that I would consider the alternatives rather than the analysis. Put in common sense terms, there are *games* and *sport.* At this point they simply cannot be differentiated analytically. Each also has a political component of whatever variety— interpersonal, structural or societal. These categories must be placed in the context of history. Thence, the grounded theory of all these vague, huge, amorphous terms may be generated. So, I bring together these studies of games, sport and power.

Sociology cannot persist without a sense of history. Today, survey research and the remarkable facility of electronic computers seem conspiratorially to rob sociology of that sense of history. Yet, paradoxically, history itself cannot be grasped without doing violence to the processes it must encompass. This is true of statistics as well. Any categorization of survey data means the loss of variation. When we view the forest, we miss the trees, and vice versa. Let us, then, look at history in terms of economic development, at the same time granting the certainty of historical error. The history of the Americas can be conceived (or misconceived) as comprised of three major stages of economic development—colonization, industrialization and high mass consumption.

We shall not here be concerned with the stage of colonization. At that time sport and games commanded what seems to be little significance for the institutional arrangements of those continents. The stage of industrialization is another matter. Here the basic economic problem of the society is production; and for the person, work. When societies industrialize, as Veblen so sardonically pointed out, sport and games are conspicuously elevated to the domain of what he called the leisure classes. A similar period has been aptly called "the bleak age" by the Hammonds in their analysis of seventeenth and eighteenth century England. I think we can apply the term to the United States in the nineteenth century and possibly to most of Middle and South America today. To apply such a term, is, of course, not to say that there was or is no play, that there were or are no games, or that there was or is no sport in that stage of economic development. But sport and many games are confined precisely to the leisure classes. As the Freudian metaphor implies, work is but accomplished to offset the burden of guilt, while play may create the very guilt that drives men to work.

Dennis Wrong has raised the question: "Is there no one who has not felt guilty about his own conformity?" He suggests, also, that people are motivated by the quest for the respect of others as well as by the internalized norms which give rise to a sense of guilt when they are violated. But I wonder, following Harry Stack Sullivan, whether the burden of respect is not as great as the burden of guilt. Sport and games really were the principal modes of distancing available to the leisure classes of the United States in its phase of industrialization. I offer the hypothesis that these were forms of activity in which leisure classes could engage to alleviate their anxiety about the respect accorded them by the masses. Nevertheless, their anxiety could not be assuaged, were they to become overly proficient in activities which were blatantly irrelevant for solving the problems posed by the economy in that stage of development, namely production and work.

Howard S. Becker has discussed commitment as established, among other things, by side bets. One's commitment to an occupation is buttressed by the obligations he builds in other areas of life—his family, his house, his church, his associations, friendships and all those other relationships which do not directly pertain to his work. Those leisure classes could not become committed to sport, even as a side bet. Their real worlds had to appear to be elsewhere. Their engagement in sports and games was really play—a conspicuously unserious part of their lives. Thus Ned Polsky reminds us of the remark, falsely attributed to Herbert Spencer: "To play a good game of billiards is a sign of a well rounded education, but to play too good a game of billiards is a sign of a misspent youth." (This was really Lord Chesterfield's warning to his son against becoming too good a flute player.) Polsky goes on to say, "The upper class must uphold the distinction between the amateur and the professional, and the true gentleman takes care that he cannot possibly be taken for a professional. . . ."

In short, the leisure classes could not be too serious about their leisure. They had to maintain a certain flexibility or "play" in such activities which could evidence to others that they were playing precisely because they were not serious. (Veblen missed this point.) They demonstrated this by "playing down" their level of competence. Perhaps this playing down of competence by the leisure classes ushered in the era of the hustler in play and games. He became a kind of protégé whose function was to dramatize the *near-competence* of the leisure classes. Polsky's material suggests this, and we also know about the history of boxing. Outstanding early boxers were pulled into early recognition by instructing the leisure classes in the *gentlemanly* art of self defense. George Bernard Shaw's novel, written in 1882, *Cashell Byron's Profession,* fictionalizes the process as it pertained in the nineteenth century, but it remains true today. Hustlers come from the masses; they hustle the classes.

Be these things as they may, in the industrial society, sport and games were "played" in the sense that I have indicated. Games and sport acted to unify the leisure classes, to alleviate their anxiety about the respect which was paid to them, and enabled them to maintain a patronizing relationship with the masses by occasionally inviting them into participation in their games and sport, or asking them to introduce their games and sport to the leisure classes.

We must also not forget, as Polsky says, that games as opposed to sport offered a way of life to those who were not quite *with* the social arrangements of the society. He points out that the demise of the pool hustler began with the decline of the single heterosexual culture in western civilization. One is reminded of Reuel Denny's query, "Whatever happened to the uncle?" in his wonderful book, *The Astonished Muse.* Do hustlers persist after uncles are gone? Is the societal lifetime of the hustler longer than the lifetime of the uncle? Entrepreneurial games such as pool and poker decline in importance as society progresses to a stage of high mass consumption. This may mean that the hustler dies the death of the uncle. His generation is consumed by the inexorable pressure of demography, reflecting, to be sure, the more basic metabolic quiverings of larger institutional arrangements. Yet, there is the matter of hustling at golf—a major hustle in the United States today. Joe Louis, it is said, was an easy mark for the golf hustler. Note, however, the different social significance of the settings in which pool and poker, as opposed to golf, are accomplished.

In the stage of high mass consumption sport is consumed. Playing at sport becomes a commodity to be consumed by spectators. Interestingly, this provides a powerful stimulus for the athlete to increase or enhance his competence. Spectators cannot be attracted to the gates of stadia or ball fields to witness mere approximations to expert performances. Players, consequently, are constrained towards excellence. Indeed, athletes achieve excellence and, as a result, become high priced commodities. The masses pay for their performances, so the masses pay for any halo effect that their heroes can be paid to bestow on other commodities. Athletes, therefore, become committed to their occupations by a proliferation of side bets—side bets totally unfamiliar to Shaw or Cashell Byron.

This is what Ralph Andreano is talking about when he speaks of the affluent baseball player. Making the athlete a commodity increases his side bets and decreases his individuality. The "characters" in professional sports disappear as the professionalization of sports, i.e., the translation of sport into commodity, takes hold. In this sense, I suppose, we can speak of sport as an opiate of the people. The people are literally mesmerized by the production of sports activities as those goods are distributed around the world by the mass media of communication. In this stage of high mass consumption the problem is that of distribution. The goods of sport are distributed on the thin waves of air that connect television antennae, whether the circuits are closed or not.

These thin waves of air are overcast by the clouds of respectability. Consequently, Ortega was not quite correct when he spoke of the revolt of the masses. The masses are not oppressed by the burden of respectability, although certainly, they want this respectability without comprehending its burden or obligations. Possibly the stimulus to revolution which seems historically to originate with the upper and upper middle strata in all the countries of the world arises from the burden of respectability. The *noblesse oblige* persists in spite of the revolt of the masses or the entry of the "hard hats" on the social, economic and political scenes. In an age of high mass consumption, where distribution is the problem and status is the reward, we may well expect that the burden of respectability will be maintained by creating an anxiety of the masses. Soccer may be a way of life for Brazilians, and ultimately an opiate of the people, but the people may well not understand where their addiction leads them.

In terms of sport and the shifts in economic development from societal problems of production to those of distribution or, in the personal mind, from work to consumption, let us metaphorize this shift as a difference between hustlers and athletes. We can see from these articles that any hustler must perfect his hustle in his early teens. This means, of course, that he cannot be distracted by such societal enticements as the educational system, what we ordinarily call school. As a matter of fact, hustlers cannot entertain the allure of side bets. A pool player plays pool; a card player plays cards. Golf hustlers may have been caddies in early adolescence. None of these, if he is a genuine entrepreneur, becomes involved with the institutions of the society—those institutions that grant status, marriage, religion or education. Hustlers must drop out of the society in their teens. This is certainly true for pool players and card sharks. Polsky demonstrates that any pool hustler must, like a concert pianist, take up his trade as a teenager. Martinez and LaFranchi in depicting types of poker players show that winners at poker are slightly younger than the "break-evens, losers or action players." Moreover these winners are more apt to be single or divorced, as opposed to other players. If one is going to hustle, one can't have too many side bets, and one must begin his hustle early.

As opposed to the hustler, who must groom himself *with* others, the athlete is groomed *by* others, for he is a commercial product. Thus, most coaches force a kind of celibacy on the athlete, as though his genitals were a source of power as the Freudians would like us to believe. Joe Namath and Dave Meggyesy have stated publicly that athletes are fed up with this. Bo Belinsky could not be allowed to make it with Mamie Van Doren, because she could obviously drain his genitals. His career represents a perfect example of what Merton has called the self-fulfilling prophecy. Repudiating the grooming destroyed his saleability as a product. The proof? He was sent down to the minors. Perhaps Dennis McLain is on the same track today.

There is another dimension, and this is brought out by Schafer and Armer with respect to the high school athlete. High school athletes consistently perform better academically than do nonathletes. This finding puts down the snobbism of sociologists who, as we have said before, are haunted by the ghosts of work, but here again we must raise the question of whether the superior academic performance is not another instance of the self-fulfilling prophecy. We know that teachers are subject to no little pressure to maintain the grades of athletes. I have even seen a case where an athletic director of a large university committed perjury in court to defend a collegiate football star in a civil suit. Yet the article by Schafer and Armer does much to raise doubts in the minds of uncritical viewers of the sport scene today. This may all be part of the larger social organization of sport in American society. As Andreano reminds us, 40 percent of the baseball players that he studied attended junior colleges, colleges or universities. Colleges and certainly high schools fashion the commodities which are sold in the big leagues.

Here there may be a backlash. When we put people in school, we forget that they might learn something. We can see this today as minds emerge out of bodies. One need only cite the struggle of Curt Flood, the writings of Jim Brosnan, Jim Bouton, Jerry Kramer, Namath, Meggyesy or even the vicarious observations of George Plimpton. The schools produce consumer goods for the world of sport. They may also give the athlete some food for thought—and the burden of respect. Although athletes may be packaged and processed by educational institutions for the consumption of spectators, this does not mean that the consumers of sport are well fed. (They do become fed up at times as indicated by the recent serious breach in diplomatic relations between Honduras and El Salvador stimulated by a soccer match.)

So play, transformed into games or sport, can be the symbol of warfare—as Goodhart and Chataway have shown in their *War Without Weapons* (London: W. R. Allen, 1968)—the unification of status circles, the alienation of societal segments, the representation of stages of economic growth, and the conning of players. Obviously, then, play carries with it the implications of power. These implications have not at all been seriously studied, but the articles we include in this volume provide some insights into the matter.

Bensman shows how the burden of respectability arranges the division of labor among concert musicians; and they do play. The arrangement is not territorial. It is purely sociological. No matter where they are, conductors esteemed by audiences and critics are given short shrift by performers. In this sense performers lose power as they perform in concerts. Conductors shoulder the burden of respectability and control orchestras. In this short article, Bensman raises all the questions I wish to reiterate, but not to answer, about power in the United States. Is there a power elite, as C. Wright Mills would have it, or is power diffused over the social body throughout an aggregation of veto groups, as David Riesman thinks? Does status or the burden of respectability confer power, or is power appropriated by military, political, economic office or any office, for that matter? Is there a daily life decided by multiple elites or by a power elite? These are questions that I invite the reader to entertain upon reading the contribution of Bensman in this volume. These are questions that I cannot answer now, but which sociologists must answer at some time and at some place. An entering wedge is certainly provided by Dan Bell's assertion that we must sort out the various types of decisions in which power is exerted.

Then there are the masses. They comprise the spectators, the audiences or the consumers of the commodities of play. Do *they* control? The players may. As Peterson points out, players of jazz educate audiences, but only to yesterday's jazz. One thinks of political rhetoric in the United States. Are not the politicians educating the voters to yesterday's ideals? Nixon has too late become a Keynesian. Well, then the creative musician succeeds. He educates the audience to yesterday, and they accept his teaching. He moves on to today and sometimes tomorrow, but then he becomes a prisoner—a prisoner of his own self, a prisoner of his own style. The educated audience then locks him into that style, and he cannot escape it. Here, the locus of power seems to be up for grabs. The debate between Riesman and Mills is suddenly revealed as empty. They talk about what is, but not about what's going on—about structure, not process.

We can get some insight into this problem by

considering Lopata and Noel on the powering of dance hall clientele, the coercion of the lonely people in the society into a routine that they never expected or could never really perform. Here is an exercise in interpersonal power that has been quite carefully scheduled by those who control the dancing of the dancers in the lonely crowd. But all of this terrible control of lonely people must be accomplished in the matrix of history. This matrix is constantly changing.

Museums, like the entire world of play, shift their purposes from elitist, royalist, devotion to the representation of a patrician past to democratic, educational and community ends. Just as sport and games changed from a representation of the status of those who engaged in them in the industrial society to a commodity for the consumption of spectators, so have museums changed their ideology. We can see this in architecture, as Graña suggests. Note *institutes* of art versus museums of *modern* art.

Finally Berger shows us that historical differences are sometimes synchronic and so reflected in space. What we think is comic has very serious implications. Our play, including our comedy, reveals fundamentally different social and social psychological orientations to authority. He compares Marmittone with Beetle Bailey, Mickey Mouse with Ignatz, the Little King with Lola, and he presumes that the problem of power or authority in the United States in the stage of high mass consumption is not quite so depressing as many think it to be.

Having said all of this, I hope that I have erected a sociological structure for the interpretation of games and sport as they vary over time and space. But, to return to Wittgenstein, I must admit that the structure is but a scaffold. Within the scaffold, the building goes on. As of this writing, though we must destroy the scaffold, the building has barely commenced.

Let me, at the end or the beginning, express my sincere appreciation to Harvey Farberman, Benjamin Lowe, Gladys Stone and Judith Woodmansee for their conjoint work, play and games which made this book possible. It was sporting of them.

Part One

GAMES

Of Pool Playing
and Poolrooms

NED POLSKY

The game of pool, or "pocket billiards" as the men who make playing equipment or run the fancier poolrooms would like you to call it, has been undergoing a renaissance. This revival, accidentally touched off by the enormous success of the movie *The Hustler* (late 1961, re-released 1964), has been kept going via an adroit and energetic public relations campaign by certain sporting equipment manufacturers, chiefly Brunswick. The manufacturers are running scared: bowling alleys have been overbuilt, and equipment makers are faced not only with declining demand but the prospect of having to repossess thousands of automatic pinsetters, costing

An earlier version of this essay appeared in *trans*action magazine, March 1967. This version is reprinted from Ned Polsky, *Hustlers, Beats and Others* (New York: Doubleday Anchor Books, 1969), pages 1-30. Copyright © 1967, 1969 by Ned Polsky. Reprinted by permission of the author and Aldine-Atherton, Inc.

$9,000 each, which they have financed on long-term notes. Thus the attempt to cash in on *The Hustler* and revive pool and billiards. The campaign just might work, for such a reversal of fashion is not without precedent in our sports history; an observer wrote in 1869 that "popular favor for ten-pins having about this time—the close of 1858—yielded to the superior attraction of billiards, Mr. Kingsley changed his alleys into a poolroom devoted to the latter game."[1]

The current upsurge in pool playing is not nearly as impressive as many press releases and planted feature stories would have one believe. Four decades ago the number of American poolrooms was four times what it is today, and on a per capita basis (number of pool and billiard tables compared with the total population) poolrooms were then about ten times as popular as they are now after three years of "revival." But there has undoubtedly been a recent growth of interest in poolroom games, after more than three decades of unrelieved decline: witness the installing of many pool and billiard tables in bowling establishments; a sharp rise in the sale of private tables to suburban homeowners; pool contests on nationwide television; and most importantly, the opening of more than 3,000 new poolrooms.[2]

As one whose chief recreation since the age of 13 has been billiards, I am as much in favor of renewed public interest in poolrooms as any professional yea-sayer in the industry. But sociological analysis of the available historical data, reported below, forces me to conclude

[1] Cf. Dudley Kavanagh, *The Billiard World* (New York: Kavanagh & Decker, 1869), p.27.

[2] For statistics on the number of poolrooms and pool and billiard tables, see note 44.

that the present revival will soon peter out, and that American per capita participation in poolroom games will never again become even a sixth of what it once was.

In this conclusion I am in sorrowful disagreement with the manufacturers and poolroom owners, who at this improved moment in their fortunes are understandably optimists almost to a man. Recollecting, as they do, the once-great popularity of poolrooms, they believe that the revival will not only be maintained but hugely expanded. Moreover, they are confident that they have hit upon a method to assure this end.

Being aware of the moral stigma attached to poolrooms, they place faith in publicly and loudly casting out sin—the method of "deviance disavowal" as the sociologist has it, or of "upgrading" one's "image" as the adman has it. In the poolroom business this process is known as "cleaning up the game," and currently it revolves about such things as installing carpets and bright lights and pastel colors, curbing obscene language, getting rid of hustlers and hoodlums and alcoholics, and trying to bring women in. On the advice of public relations counsel, the trade has also given outward and visible sign of the inward and spiritual grace by undergoing rebaptism: "poolrooms" have been replaced by "billiard lounges."[3]

Lately the trade has, in addition, made use of public relations men in the latter's role as inventors and

---

[3] In an earlier attempt to reduce stigma, just before the turn of the century, many "poolrooms" and "poolhalls" became "billiard academies." But the effectiveness of this substitute—if any—soon wore off, as often happens with euphemisms. On the "wearing out" of euphemisms, cf. Leonard Bloomfield, *Language* (New York: Henry Holt, 1933), p. 410.

purveyors of conscious, deliberate falsehoods.[4] To give but one example: the 1963 world professional pocket billiard (pool) tournament saw the emergence of a new champion, Luther Lassiter, who later won the 1964 tournament as well. Now the central face of Lassiter's previous occupational life is that he had been for many years, under the monicker of "Wimpy," a genuine pool hustler of the old school—indeed such a good one that many of his hustler colleagues had long acknowledged his supremacy in one form of the grift, the game of nine ball. But the public relations men who now write of Lassiter alternately suppress and blatantly deny this, and their fabrications are conveyed to mass audiences by reporters who conceive of journalism as the rephrasing of press handouts (see, for example, the mindless article on pool in the *Saturday Evening Post* of April 19, 1964).

In this access of real and imagined virtue the manufacturers and poolroom owners are proceeding, I think, on a mistaken assumption. They subscribe to the commonly accepted view that the game's popularity waned because of the growing association of poolrooms, in the public mind, with gamblers, loafers, criminals and the like. It seems to me that the historical evidence reveals this explanation to be dead wrong, and that poolrooms instead declined because of certain long-term

---

[4] This sort of thing poses ticklish research problems in any study that must, like this one, draw upon mass periodicals for some source material. Over four-fifths of the news items in the modern newspaper, and the large majority of articles in most mass magazines, derive from material supplied by public relations men, publicity men, official press representatives and the like—men whose jobs require them to serve with extraordinary frequency as professional liars.

changes in America's social structure that are, apparently, irreversible.

The historical evidence on pool or any other sport is not conveniently "given" and merely awaiting sociological analysis. In this regard the sociologist, concerned with tracing how the history of an American sport is related to such things as social structure and social change, finds himself confronted with two unanticipated research problems.

His first special problem is that America's professional historians have not done what might be deemed their part of the job. Some of their works on various historical periods give, to be sure, once-over-lightly accounts of sports and games popular at different times; and they have written surveys of American sports history as such, the most notable being John Krout's *Annals of American Sport* (1929) and Foster Rhea Dulles' *America Learns to Play* (1940). But except possibly for baseball, the grand total of professional historical writing on any particular sport does not begin to resemble a reasonably detailed and reliable history of that sport—whether social history or any other kind.

A related problem is that amateurs have rushed in where professionals fear to tread, and have set many traps for the unwary researcher. Much published material that calls itself history of this or that sport is, in considerable part, nonsense. It may be found in the introductory sections or appendices of instruction manuals on sports, in encyclopedia articles, and in specialized periodicals about sports. The writer of such "history" sometimes is professionally connected with the sport, sometimes is a devoted fan, but in any case is not trained to do historical research. Some of his material is unavoidably important and must be drawn upon, especially if it gives an eyewitness account behind which one can detect no ulterior motive or sloppiness or undue play of the writer's imagination. But even when written out of purest intent, almost invariably this material contains much that is demonstrably wrong.

Quite representative of the genre are the historical discussions in the two latest billiard instruction books.[5] Their accounts of events beyond living memory are uncritically compiled from secondary sources and repeat errors that infest even the best of these sources (such as the *Encyclopaedia Britannica* and Frank Menke's *New Encyclopedia of Sports*). They tell us, for example, that billiards entered America about 1565 when Spaniards brought a form of the game to St. Augustine; but my own research on the American history of billiards has failed to uncover any reference before the late seventeenth century. The notion that the American game began over a century earlier is a myth passed on from one lazy billiard historian to the next; hardly one of them has ever bothered his head about finding a primary source for the alleged fact of sixteenth-century origin, which isn't surprising when you consider that most such "historians" don't know there is such a distinction between primary and secondary sources.[6]

---

[5] Cf. the historical sections in Luther Lassiter, *The Modern Guide to Pocket Billiards* (New York: Fleet Publishing Co., 1964), and in Clive Cottingham, Jr., *The Game of Billiards* (Philadelphia: Lippincott & Co., 1965).

[6] An honorable exception, who is not faultless but sees some of the myths for what they are, is the anonymous author of *Modern Billiards* (New York: Brunswick-Balke-Collender Co., 1908), pp. 5-6. His warnings have gone unheeded by later writers on billiard history except Louise Belden, *op. cit infra*, note 31.

The real pity in the lunkhead tradition of cobbling together secondary material is that just a little original searching reveals all sorts of useful data never cited by any sports historian, amateur or professional. Let us look at some of these data.

As soon as one begins seriously to examine primary sources, the standard explanation for the decline of poolrooms collapses. Material from every historical period reveals one fact overwhelmingly: poolrooms *always* had "middle-class morality" very solidly against them, were *always* highly stigmatized. This opposition to public poolrooms even extended, on occasion, to private playing at home by the ultrarespectable. When President John Quincy Adams installed a billiard table in the White House (with his own money), his opponents in Congress were able to raise a big stink about this acquiring of "gambling furniture" and to use the purchase as campaign material against him in the election of 1828.[7]

Literally hundreds of sources showed that, in America, from the very beginning and uninterruptedly throughout their history, public poolrooms (which started out as taverns and roadside inns), were always associated with gambling and various forms of low life; ministers were always denouncing them, police were always finding wanted criminals in them, and parents were always warning their children to stay out of them. Here, for example, is Jerome Keogh, world's pool champion five times between 1897 and 1910, reminiscing about the 1890s:

[7]Cf. Samuel Flagg Bemis, *John Quincy Adams and the Union* (New York: Alfred A. Knopf, 1956), p. 94.

Despite the vaunted glamour of the great billiard academies of the gay nineties . . . the fact was that during this period "nice" young men stole surreptitiously through the by-ways of the night to enter them, lest detection should result in the stigma of being "fast." . . . the game struggled against the dictates of society, the raising of eyebrows, and the word "pool" uttered with caustic venom.[8]

Moreover, poolrooms grew steadily in popularity despite the fact that, at times, opposition to them was far more severe than that encountered during the era of their decline. In some parts of the country there were periods when they could not even advertise their existence but had to remain hidden from passing view and draw their customers strictly by word of mouth. When playwright William Dunlap of New York visited Baltimore in 1806, for example, he wrote home as follows:

I have seen several counting houses open on sunday with the clarks at work; & Billiard tables publicky notefied by sign boards. From the first I onely infer that less attention is paid to appearances here than to the northward; & from the second that gambling is not in such *general* disrepute.[9]

It is true that England exported billiards to America with no stigma attached to it. Billiards entered America as "the gentleman's game." But at home in England, the social context of billiard playing had long been more

[8] Quoted in Russell J. Phillips, "Jerome Keogh Opens Palatial Room in Rochester, New York," *Billiards Magazine* (Chicago), June, 1932, pp. 14-15.

[9] Diary of William Dunlap *(New York: New York Historical Society, 1930), Vol. 2, p. 376.*

complex than that oft-quoted phrase reveals. It is instructive to look at this complexity, because it foreshadowed similar developments that began in America soon after billiards arrived.

Much of early English billiard history is obscure, and much of what Englishmen have written about it is absurd—one unfortunate parallel with America being that English professional historians have also left the subject to incompetent amateurs.[10] But the main point of that history for our purposes is clear enough: billiard playing in England involved two separate, equally important traditions.

The first in point of time, and the one exported to America, consisted of "respectable" playing by the upper class, which flourished especially in country

---

[10]No English billiard historian has even compiled a half-way reliable bibliography of his subject. Some (by no means all) of the most serious bibliographical problems are as follows:

(1) The best-known early British book on billiards, F. White's *The Game of Billiards* (London: W. Miller, 1807), seems on internal evidence to be largely an unacknowledged translation of a French manual, but no one has tried to confirm this or even taken account of the internal evidence. (2) English billiard historians unanimously, and American counterparts with one exception, agree that White's is the first English-language book on billiards (see, for example, the *Encyclopaedia Britannica*). They are wrong. (3) The exception is Louise Belden, *op. cit. infra*, note 31, who cites a book by John Dew as *"Treatise on the Game of Billiards* (London, 1799)." But as a separately issued publication, Dew's treatise seems to be a ghost. I cannot find it in the catalogues of the British Museum, Ashley Library, London Library, Patent Office (London), Edinburgh University Library, Library of Congress, and Bibliothéque Nationale, nor in the National Union Catalogue, nor in Robert Watt's *Bibliotheca Britannica* nor in the lists of new books in the *Gentleman's Magazine* for 1799 and the *Annual Register* for 1799. (4) But

houses.[11] It is difficult to determine the dates of
country-house billiard rooms because such rooms were
often additions, i.e., were converted from rooms initially devoted to other uses, and because the original
architectural plans (unlike the ground plans published
much later in guidebooks) almost never label the use for
each room.[12] But there were some billiard rooms of this
sort in the last quarter of the sixteenth century. The
inventory of Howard House made in 1588 lists "a
billyard bord covered with a green cloth with a frame of
beache with fower turned postes," and also "three
billyard stickes and 11 balles of yvery"; and in the same
year the Earl of Leicester's goods at Wanstead, as listed
for probate, included "a billiarde table with the tools

there is another book earlier than White's, cited by no one, in the
British Museum. It is an anonymous work ("By an Amateur") of
72 duodecimo pages entitled *Game of Billiards* (London: T.
Hurst, 1801). And in it, p. [10], is a reference to playing
instructions "laid down by Mr. Dew." (5) A still earlier English
book on billiards was almost certainly published in 1772; the
"Catalogue of New Publications" in the *Gentleman's Magazine*
for that year (Vol. 42, p. 140) has this entry:

> The Odds of the Game of Billiards; accurately calculated by a
> Gentleman who has studied them many Years. To which are
> added some observations on the Game, that should be attended
> by every Player. 12mo. 1s. Bladon.

The book is also listed in *Bibliotheca Britannica*. Apparently no
copy of this 1772 volume survives.

The bibliography of British writing on billiards to be found
elsewhere than in billiard books (e.g., periodicals, diaries, general
books on sports and games) is in still worse shape—but I have no
space to deal with this.

[11] Among early guidebooks to country houses that mention
billiard rooms are the following: Anon., *Aedes Pembrochianae:
Being a New and Critical Account . . . of the Antiquities at
Wilton-House* (London: R. Baldwin, 1744), p. 45; J. Seeley,

appurteyninge."[13] Other country-house billiard rooms
which available information indicates are both original
and early include those at Burghley House (completed
1589), Bramshill (completed 1612), Knole (completed
1608), Dorton House (completed 1626), and Hatfield
House (completed 1611).[14]

Although the billiard room was as richly appointed as
any other in the country house—with, for example,

Stowe:A Description of the House and Gardens (Buckingham:
The Author, 1797), pp. 43, 49 (Stowe had two billiard rooms; its
two regular billiard tables are listed in the sale catalogue of 1848,
and another, miniature, billiard table is listed in the sale catalogue
of 1921); Anon., *A History and Description ... of Burghley
House* (Shrewsbury: J. and W. Eddowes, 1797), p. 126; D.
Jacques, *A Visit to Goodwood* (Chichester: The Author, 1822),
pp. 48, 52 (Goodwood had two billiard rooms); Anon., *A
Description of Hagley, Envil, and the Leasowes* (Birmingham:
The Author, n.d. [*ca.* 1765]), p. 136; John Britton, *Graphic
Illustrations of Toddington* (London: The Author, 1840), plates
[1] and [16] (the latter plate illustrates Toddington's billiard
room); John Young, *Catalogue of the Pictures at Leigh Court,
Near Bristol* (London: The Proprietor, 1822), p. 27; John Brady,
The Visitor's Guide to Knole ... (Sevenoaks: James Payne,
1839), p. 125; William Dean, *An Historical and Descriptive
Account of Croome D'Abitot* (Worcester: T. Eaton, 1824), p. 50
(description of the billiard room); Anon., *An Historical and
Descriptive Account of Stoke Park in Buckinghamshire* (London:
W.Bulmer, 1813), p. [79].
[12] But cf. James Gibbs, *A Book of Architecture containing
Designs of Buildings and Ornaments*, 2d ed. (London: W. Innys
and R. Manby, 1739), p. xiii and plate XLVIII.
[13] Quoted from "Tables, Billiard," in Ralph Edwards (Ed.),
Dictionary of English Furniture, 2d ed. (London: Country Life,
1954), pp. 187 ff.; this article is in every respect the best account
of early billiard history in England. Note that these 1588
quotations slightly antedate the *O.E.D.*'s first record of the word
"billiards" in the English language (1591).
[14] Anon., *Guide to Burghley House, Stamford* (Stamford: Doby

paintings by such artists as Holbein, Canaletto and Van
Dyck—the table itself was often of great interest to
visitor and owner alike. Thus John Evelyn, in his
seventeenth-century diary, carefully noted the billiard
tables in the houses he visited. In 1844 the Duke of
Devonshire proudly described his table at Chatsworth as
follows:

> The Billiard-table, made by Thurston, full size—
> which means that there is still a fuller size—is suited
> to the smallness of the room. . . . The table, of
> birds-eye maple, is a chef d'oeuvre of workmanship,
> and has been pronounced excellent by no less a man
> than "Jonathan" [a famous player of the time.][15]

Among the prize-winning examples of English craftsmanship at the Great Exhibition of 1851 were two
billiard tables (by different manufacturers) with elaborate marquetry and other ornamentation.[16]

By the time of Robert Kerr's *The Gentleman's House;
Or, How to Plan English Residences* (first edition, 1864;
third edition, 1871), it was taken for granted that any
house of reasonable size should have a billiard room,
and Kerr devoted a good deal of attention to the

Brothers, 1933), p. 19; William Cope, *Bramshill: Its History and
Architecture* (London: H. J. Infield, n.d. [after 1875], p. 36; H.
Avray Tipping, *English Homes: Late Tudor and Early Stuart,
1558-1649* (London: Country Life, 1929), p. 246; James
Hakewell, *An Attempt to Determine the Exact Character of
Elizabethan Architecture*, 2d ed. (London: John Weale, 1936), p.
[30]; Robert Kerr, *The Gentleman's House*, 3rd ed. (London:
John Murray, 1871), plate 9.
[15] Anon. [Duke of Devonshire], *Handbook of Chatsworth and
Hardwick* (London: Privately printed, n.d. [1844]), p. 35.
[16] Color lithographs of these tables comprise plate 190 of the
exhibition catalogue. Among the more notable English tables
preserved is the present one at Burghley House, whose mountings

matter.[17] So did some of the Victorian manuals on billiards.[18]

From the beginning, billiard tables also were installed in some other meeting places of the upper class. Most important of these, perhaps, were the two billiard tables in the New Assembly Rooms at Bath (built 1769-1771).[19] Some upper-class coffee houses also had billiard tables—starting with Colsini's Chocolate House, which had two billiard tables by 1693, and ending with the Smyrna Coffee House in St. James's Street, which advertised itself in 1801 as a place where "Gentlemen meet on purpose to play billiards."[20]

---

are of oak from the Royal George, sunk at Spithead in 1782. A table from about 1660, now in the Victoria and Albert Museum, is illustrated in Ralph Edwards, *op. cit.;* Probably the oldest English table extant is the one at Knole. It is illustrated in Tipping, *op. cit.,* and Edwards, *op. cit.;* its construction is briefly discussed in Margaret Jourdain, *Stuart Furniture at Knole* (London: Country Life, 1952), p. 13. Edwards, following Tipping, dates it around 1690, but I think Jourdain correctly dates the base of it about a century earlier.

[17] The construction of billiard rooms in English country houses continued well into the present century. For photographs of billiard rooms in houses not already cited, consult the files of *Country Life* and also Charles Latham's *In English Homes* (London: Country Life) as follows: Vol. 1 (1904), pp. 24, 56, 348, 365, 405; Vol. 2 (1907), pp. 166, 359, 431; Vol. 3 (1909), pp. 412, 414.

[18] See especially the lovely architectural elevations for Greek Revival and Tudor billiard annexes attached to mansions, in William Dufton's *Practical Billiards* (London: George Routledge, 1873), plates 2, 3, 4, and 5.

[19] See the floor plan in Mowbray A. Green, *The Eighteenth Century Architecture of Bath* (Bath: George Gregory, 1904), p. 161.

[20] Cf. Bryant Lillywhite, *London Coffee Houses* (London: George Allen and Unwin, 1963), entries numbered 7, 500, 1178, 1223 and 1604.

But if billiards could be played in public places
frequented by gentlemen, there was little to prevent it
being played in public places frequented by the not-so-
gentlemanly; and little did prevent it. This new type of
English billiard playing, which represented a "trickling
down" of the upper-class pastime, appears to have been
already well under way in the seventeenth century, to
judge from Charles Cotton's remarks of 1674:

> The Gentile, cleanly and ingenious game at Bil-
> liards . . . is much approved of and played by most
> Nations in *Europe,* especially in *England* there being
> few Towns of note therein which hath not a publick
> Billiard-table, neither are they wanting in many Noble
> and private Families in the Country.[21]

As this second tradition developed, the "respectable"
upper class who played at home or in meeting places
restricted to their own kind (Bath, private clubs, etc.)
were immediately concerned to distinguish themselves
from it, and in doing so they conceived it as morally
deviant. In their view, it was bad enough that *hoi aristoi*
had occasionally spent too much time and money
gambling at billiards amongst themselves (Edmund
Spenser's complaint of 1591)[22] but much worse that
hoi polloi should now become wastrels over it and even
(worst of all) sometimes seduce their weaker-minded
betters into joining with them in a life of dissolute
gaming. That is why even as early as 1674 Charles
Cotton, for all his remarks about "The Gentile, cleanly

---

[21] Gamester [Charles Cotton], *The compleat Gamester; or,
Instructions how to play at billiards, trucks, bowls and
chess. . . .* (London: Henry Brome, 1674), p. 23.
[22] "With all the thriftless games that may be found. . . . With dice,
with cards, with billiards." *Mother Hubberd's Tale* (1591).

and most ingenious game at Billiards," had to leaven his book with remarks such as these:

Mistake me not, it is not my intention to make Gamesters.

This restless man (the miserable Gamester) is the proper subject of every man's pity. Restless I call him, because (such is the itch of play) either winning or losing he can never be satisfied, if he wins he thinks to win more, if he loses he hopes to recover.

To conclude, let me advise you, if you play (when your business will permit) let not a covetous desire of winning another's money engage you to the losing of your own.[23]

As billiards spread downward from the upper class, these kinds of warnings increased in frequency and severity. There were also occasional efforts to go beyond moral suasion and legally clamp down on public billiard playing by the lower strata, such as this attempt in the Dublin of 1744:

At the Court of *King's Bench,* in *Ireland,* were convicted 15 of the Billiard Tables, presented by the Grand Jury of *Dublin,* (who had traversed) The Citizens have determin'd to prosecute, in the same Manner, all Billiard Tables that shall be erected for the Future, or those which now remain, if kept open after 9 o'Clock at Night, or knowingly suffer Merchants, Apprentices or Clerks belonging to Gentlemen of any Business, to play in their Houses.[24]

These attempts, whether in England or Ireland, succeeded only rarely and temporarily. But in any case there had developed, in addition to the approved

---

[23] Charles Cotton, *op. cit.*, pp. [vi], [vii-viii], 3.
[24] "Historical Chronicle," *Gentleman's Magazine*, Vol. 14 (1744), p. 337.

"gentleman's game" played in country houses, public billiard playing by nongentlemen that was heavily stigmatized.

In America as in England, billiards began at the top. It came as a direct importation from the English upper class to the American upper class. For example, one of the earliest genuine references to billiards in America reveals that the Colonial statesman William Byrd of Westover—who was educated in England and called to the bar at the Middle Temple—had a billiard table: in his diary entry for 30 July 1710, Byrd writes, apropos of having laid his wife, "It is to be observed that the flourish was performed on the billiard table."[25] On September 26, 1725, I find the Colonial Governor of New York, George Clinton, writing to Cadwallader Colden that "I . . . gave orders for my Billiard tables to be Set up."[26] By 1768, according to an account written in that year, the demand for billiard playing equipment was already so great that cue sticks manufactured along the James River in Virginia were being exported all the way to Boston.[27] (Despite sharply increasing demand over the next 150 years, this early American industry died out in Virginia, presumably because of the realization that the most warp-resistant woods for cue sticks are the extremely hard varieties of maple which flourish much further north.[28]

---

[25] Cf. Louis B. Wright and Marion Tinling (Eds.), *Secret Diary of William Byrd of Westover, 1709-1712* (Richmond, Va.: Dietz Press, 1941), p. 207.

[26] Cf. *Letters and Papers of Cadwallader Colden.* Vol. IX: *Additional Letters and Papers*, 1749-1775 (New York: New York Historical Society, 1937), p. 122.

[27] Cf. *Virginia Gazette*, March 3, 1768, p. 3, col. 1.

[28] Cue sticks are usually 56½ to 57 inches long, the better ones

The better-off merchant of the times could avail himself of such offerings as this one in the New York *Royal Gazette* of October 24, 1781:

To be let a new house in an excellent stand for business, it has a good cellar, two rooms below, a large billiard room above, a bed chamber, a large garret, a back kitchen, and a convenient back yard. . . .

And early American newspapers also contain quite a few advertisements addressed to the upper class along the lines of this one from the *Minerva & Mercantile Advertiser* of February 12, 1795:

William King, Ivory and Wood Turner, Informs the citizens . . . that he has commenced the turning busi-

---

being take-down models comprising two pieces of equal length, a butt and a shaft, joined via an inset brass female screw in the bottom of the shaft and a brass male screw and bushing in the top of the butt. The relatively thick butt can be made of any of various heavy woods (e.g., my own is of West African black ebony) and traditionally has a good deal of marquetry using inlays of ivory, colored woods, and mother-of-pearl. But the shaft, since it tapers to a width of only 12½ to 13½ millimeters throughout the last several inches of its length, must, if it is to resist warping, be an unadorned piece of very hard maple, turned so that the grain runs straight down the shaft, from stock that has been thoroughly kiln-dried. To produce maple shafts that are all of first quality—a criterion ignored by the newer stick-makers one must also take care to use only the heartwood near the center of the log (for which last information I am indebted to the best of the old cue-stick craftsmen, octogenarian Herman Rambow of Chicago).

Although the best kind of maple for cue sticks does not grow in England, an English variety of ash is virtually as warp-resistant. Consequently most English cue sticks are made of ash. (For this information I am indebted to the London billiard firm of Burroughes and Watts, Ltd.)

ness. . . . Billiard balls made at the shortest notice . . .

Upper-class billiard playing long survived the Colonial era. For instance, the education typically given a scion of wealth in the mid-nineteenth century was described accurately, albeit sarcastically, by Charles Nordhoff in 1868 as follows:

> J. Augustus . . . was of course in due time sent to college, where he acquired the proper proficiency in Greek, Latin, and Mathematics, slang, billiards, and brandy smashes.[29]

In fact, the British tradition of upper-class participation in billiards has in America had a continuous, if latterly rather modest, history.[30] A good many illustrious Americans have played billiards. And today the members of the Billiard Room Proprietors Association, Billiard Players Association, and the Billiard Congress of America tirelessly cite such personages in the hope that this will improve their "image." But their hope is misplaced, for they thoroughly misunderstand the relation of billiards to upper-class life.

In the first place, genteel upper-class billiard playing in America, as in England, was insulated from the rest of

---

[29] Charles Nordhoff, "Maud Elbert's Love Match" in his *Cape Cod and All Along the Shore: Stories* (New York: Harper and Brothers, 1868), p. 217.

[30] See especially the house organs and archieves of upper-class men's clubs with billiard rooms. The first national amateur billiard tournament was organized by the Racquet and Tennis Club of New York in 1887. A good account of the billiard enthusiasts in nineteenth-century clubland is A. L. Ranney, M.D., "A Historical Sketch of Amateur Billiards," in *Amateur Billiard Championship of America (Class A)—Souvenir of the First Tournament Given Under the Auspices of the Amateur Athletic Union of the United States* (New York: Knickerbocker Athletic Club, 1899), pp. 7-24.

society, and its rise and fall have followed a dynamic of their own. What professional players and poolroom owners conveniently ignore is that "the gentleman's game," to the extent that gentlemen really played it, throughout its history has had precious little to do with public poolrooms, but instead has been restricted to the billiard rooms of private men's clubs and private homes.[31] And the upper class knows what this means even if the professionals don't. The point of the remark falsely attributed to Herbert Spencer, "To play a good game of billiards is the sign of a well-rounded education, but to play too good a game of billiards is the sign of a mis-spent youth," is precisely the point made in that *locus classicus* for the ideology of the "gentleman," Lord Chesterfield's letters to his son, when Chesterfield warns his son against becoming too good a flute player: the upper class must uphold the distinction between the amateur and the professional, and the true gentleman takes care that he cannot possibly be mistaken for a professional or vice versa.

---

[31] For one of the more interesting examples in the American private home, see the photograph of the billiard room designed about 1900 by Louis Tiffany for his country estate, The Briars, Long Island, in Robert Koch, *Louis C. Tiffany: Rebel in Glass* (New York: Crown Publishers, 1964), p. 183. See also C. V. Boyd, "Billiard Room of a Country House," *Suburban Life*, Vol. 18 (January 1914), pp. 10-12.

The earliest surviving billiard table of American manufacture, made in Maryland between 1790 and 1810, is in the Winterthur Museum. A picture of it, and background information are in Louise C. Belden, "Billiards in America Before 1830," *Antiques*, Vol. 87, No. 1 (January 1965), pp. 99-101. Miss Belden's is easily the best writing on its subject heretofore published, but is more restricted than its title indicates: it deals exclusively with upper-class billiard history, and in a limited way (e.g., using none of the pre-1830 material from the upper class that I have quoted).

This moral has never been lost on the American billiard-playing elite, and the traditional attempts of professional pool and billiard players to identify themselves with such circles, e.g., by wearing tuxedos when appearing in professional tournaments, are merely pathetic. To be sure, a Luther Lassiter or a Willie Mosconi may be invited to give an exhibition before the assembled members of a men's club—a comedown from the days when Willie Hoppe gave command performances for presidents and royalty, but still something. And if the professional should need money in his later years he may even end his days in their permanent employ (for example, the old balk-line billiard champion Jake Schaefer, Jr., has for some time run the billiard room of the Cleveland Athletic Club). But it is all part of the relation of master to hired performer. Even Willie Hoppe, who was a real stuffed shirt and tried his damnedest to dissociate himself from the poolroom subculture (he didn't even smoke or drink), for all his wealth and gentlemanly yearnings and polite manners never quite made it in the upper class as an equal.

In the past, major poolrooms did indeed manage to attract some upper-class patrons, not only *nouveaux riches* businessmen but occasional scions of old wealthy families as well. However, such people were a different breed from the gentlemen who played at the Union League or at home over cigars and sherry, and in fact constituted the most disreputable segment of the upper class. One of the latent functions of the American poolroom, like the racetrack in many of its phases, was as a place where the "sporting" fringe of the upper class—the hedonists and hellraisers given to heavy drinking and gambling and whoring—could get together with the "sporting element" of the lower class and lower-middle class to the exclusion of those who subscribed to "middle-class morality." [32] Poolrooms were major gathering places for the sporting fraternity and served them in various ways; for instance, in the early 1920s, Jack Doyle's Billiard Academy was the place where the daily "line" (more or less official bookmakers' odds) was determined for every sports event in New York City.[33]

What used to be called "sporting life," the orientation of leisure around a set of hedonistic and deviant concerns, has in America not died out or even diminished. Rather, it has retained many of its old institutional forms (bookies and racetracks, orgies and stag shows, after-hours liquor-cum-gambling joints, cocaine, bars where prostitutes are permitted or encouraged to operate, floating crap and card games), while sloughing

---

[32] For example, see the further remarks of Keogh in Russell Phillips, *op. cit.*, p. 15. Public billiard rooms in England of course had a similar function; cf. Edward Russell Mardon, *Billiards: Game 500 Up. Played at Brighton, on the 18th of January, 1844. A Description of the Above Game, with Diagrams Shewing the Position of the Balls for the Last Nine Breaks* (Brighton: W. Leppard, n.d. [1844]), pp. 4, 102-103.

Many criminologists believe that if we had accurate statistics on victim crime (including a proper accounting of white-collar crime), we would find a sharply bimodal distribution of such crime by social class, with the least of it in the middle class. See especially Walter Reckless, *The Crime Problem*, 2nd ed. (New York: Appleton-Century-Crofts, 1955), pp. 28-30. My point about the latent functions of poolrooms and racetracks is that the same pattern also seems true of the "vices," that is, non-victim crime and legal but morally stigmatized behavior.

[33] For this information on Doyle's Academy I am indebted to my father, Joseph Polsky.

off some others (poolrooms, whorehouses, opium, burlesque houses) and developing some new ones (call-girl organizations operating through model agencies and escort services, marijuana, the gambling centers of Lake Tahoe and Las Vegas, free-lance call girls operating via telephone-answering services, phenomenally increased gambling at golf). It remains to be explained why poolrooms got lost in the shuffle.

One answer sometimes given, and at first glance an appealing one, has to do not with the poolroom's latent functions but its manifest functions: a place where one plays or watches pool and billiards. It is occasionally said that pool and billiards were killed by other sports, especially the rise of mass participation in bowling and mass spectatorship for professional football.

It has been claimed apropos of the first that, relative to bowling, pool and billiards are too hard to learn well. The argument goes that thousands of regular bowlers can work up to an average of 180 or better, but that getting to the point in pool where you can average nearly ten balls an inning and occasionally run more than 50, or to the point in three-cushion billiards where you can average nearly one an inning and occasionally run more than seven, is a very much more difficult matter.

There are some genuine grains of truth at the bottom of this argument. Outstanding pool or billiard play requires thousands of hours of practice, and, to boot, early entry, as much as outstanding piano playing does. I have never met or heard of a really first-class pool or billiard player who was not playing regularly by his early teens. An additional fact supporting this position, though it seems never to have been adduced, is that many of the greatest pool and billiard players, probably the majority, started training well before their teens because they were sons of poolroom owners (e.g., Ralph Greenleaf, Willie Hoppe, Babe Cranfield, Jay Bozeman, Willie Mosconi, Welker Cochran) and in one case the son of a professional player (Jake Schaefer, Jr.). But this entire line of argument really doesn't hold up, for it assumes that true enjoyment of the game depends on attaining to the level of the top one-fifth of 1 percent of players. The fact is that millions of Americans have greatly enjoyed playing pool regularly even though they have never come close to running 50 balls—have enjoyed it just as much as, say, the millions of golfers who have never broken 80 have enjoyed playing golf. And as we saw earlier, in the 1850s billiards in fact superseded bowling in popularity; there seems to be no reason intrinsic to these games themselves why such a reversal couldn't happen again.

The second point of view sees a shift in spectator sports interests as perhaps the chief villain in the piece. For example, Willie Mosconi has recalled that, in Chicago in the early 1930s, it was common for him to draw 1500 spectators to a Saturday night pool exhibition while the Chicago Bears would draw 1200 the next day.[34] It is undeniably true that from about 1930 on poolrooms steadily declined while, during the Depression era, spectator interest in football, basketball, etc., began slowly to rise; and it is also true that as the Depression eased, most Depression-hurt sports made recoveries but pool and billiards declined very much more. However, there is no evidence of a real cause-and-effect relationship here. Pool and billiards have

---

[34] Cf. Mosconi as quoted in the New York *Post*, December 18, 1961, p. 62.

always had plenty of competition for spectators (and players) from any number of other sports and games, and did quite well nonetheless.

Similarly, it is illogical to blame the decline of poolrooms on the spread of radios, automobiles and the movies.[35] There is no evidence whatsoever that their negative effect on poolroom attendance was any greater than that provided by the many popular diversions which existed in the palmy days of the poolroom (such as the home phonograph and player piano, vaudeville and the legitimate theatre, public dance halls and ballrooms, taverns, racetracks and so on).

And if mass spectatorship for sports has any relevance as such, then the post-1945 role of television in fantastically increasing that spectatorship should, if anything, have helped pool and billiards even more than most other sports. For a pool or billiard game is ideal for TV: it is not as spread out and hard to follow on television as football or baseball, and when the camera looks down on the table from a reasonably steep angle (as it usually does), the home viewer gets a truer picture of the game than even the front-row spectators do. Yet television did nothing to revive pool and billiards; such games did not become TV fare until mid-1963, after the revival was well under way.

Finally, one should note that although the current poolroom revival is already exhibiting danger signs (more on this below), the sale of small-sized pool tables to home-owners is still sharply increasing. The ups and downs of poolrooms, as we shall see, have had not so much to do with pool as with poolrooms.

---

[35] As, for example, Robert Coughlan does in his "Pool: Its Players and Its Sharks," *Life*, Vol. 3l, No. 15 (October 8, 1951), p. 166.

As we have observed, the various alleged "causes" for the decay of the American poolroom have had a minor role at best. The genuine prime cause seems never to have been mentioned: poolrooms were the exact center and veritable stronghold of a special kind of subculture that has become increasingly rare and unimportant in America—the heterosexual but all-male subculture, which required that certain gathering places (clubs, barber shops, taverns) serve as sacrosanct refuges from women. The poolroom was not just one of these places: it was *the* one, the keystone.

The once-great attraction of pool and billiards, both for spectators and players, was in large part factitious; it had not so much to do with the games themselves as with the poolroom's latent function as the greatest and most determinedly all-male institution in American social life. The poolroom got so thoroughly bound up with this function that it could not readily adapt itself to changed conditions; when the subculture died, the poolroom nearly died with it.

To see the true dimensions of this historical drift, one must realize that the old poolroom depended not merely, or even primarily, on the equivalent of today's audience of unmarried teenagers combined with husbands out for a weekly "night with the boys" or playing at lunchtime, but on people who spent far more time than these in the poolroom: adult men who were heterosexual but nevertheless committed to remaining unmarried. Moreover, the ideology of this bachelor subculture spilled over to married life itself; that is, married men spent more nights "out with the boys" than they do today, which of course further helped poolroom attendance. (Both the "pure" and the "married" subcultural types linger in the nation's historical consciousness, or nostalgia, via highly anachronistic comic-strip characters; Moon Mullins pre-eminently represents the first type, while the second is notably represented by Mutt and by Major Hoople.)[36]

As everyone appears to know thanks to Kinsey, if an American male over the age of 35 has never been married there is a strong chance that he is actively and primarily homosexual.[37] But what everyone seems to forget is that this is a major change in the odds and represents a recent shift in America's sexual history. For various reasons connected with our country's economic development and its historic patterns of immigration, not too long ago the heterosexual confirmed bachelor was a common American social type. For example, the bachelor "uncle"—sometimes a real uncle, sometimes an honorary one, but in any event a bachelor—was a fixture in hundreds of thousands of American families. He may not have been very active sexually, but his sexual activity, such as it was, was rarely homosexual. (I am talking about overt behavior only; what existed in repressed form may be another story.) His sexual needs

---

[36] Married pool players given to frequent nights "out with the boys" are most fully delineated in Clare Briggs' cartoon feature, *Kelly Pool*, which appeared regularly in the sports section of the New York *Tribune* from 1912 to 1917. (For recollecting and calling my attention to these cartoons I am indebted to my father, Joseph Polsky.)

[37] Among unmarried American males 35 or older with at least a ninth-grade education, about 42 per cent have at least as much homosexual experience per year as heterosexual experience; among those with less than a ninth-grade education, about 28 per cent have at least as much homosexual experience per year as heterosexual experience. Cf. Alfred Kinsey, Wardell Pomeroy, and Clyde Martin, *Sexual Behavior in the Human Male* (Philadelphia: W. B. Saunders Co., 1948), p. 644, fig. 164.

were met throughout his life partly by masturbation and partly or mainly by regular recourse to professional whores. Today American men use whores pre-maritally, extra-maritally, and post-maritally, but hardly ever any more as a way of maintaining lifelong bachelorhood.[38]

Curiously, American historians seem never to have assayed, indeed seem to be oblivious of, the swiftly growing role of a confirmed-bachelor subculture in the social history of nineteenth-century America. Yet the evidence is plain enough.

For one thing, a number of American institutions whose palmy days were in the later nineteenth or early twentieth century immediately reveal themselves, once their histories are examined, as having drawn sustenance from that subculture and often, indeed, having been part and parcel of it—not only the poolroom, but institutions as various as the IWW, lodges and other fraternal organizations, red-light districts, middle-class and upper-class men's clubs, boarding houses, tramp and hobo life. Secondly, there increasingly emerged, in the lowbrow and middlebrow literature of the times, much that gave bachelors a consciousness of kind and gave ideological expression to permanent bachelorhood (as in the *Police Gazette*, whose formerly vital role in our popular culture is hard to appreciate now). Thirdly, the most sophisticated compilation of historical statistics on

---

[38]In this connection note the Kinsey data, which reveal that although the percentage of males born after 1900 who visited prostitutes was not significantly different from the percentage among males born earlier, the frequency with which they made such visits had been reduced to about half what it was in the pre-1900 generation. Cf. Alfred Kinsey, Wardell Pomeroy, Clyde Martin, and Paul Gebhard, *Sexual Behavior in the Human Female* (Philadelphia: W. B. Saunders Co., 1953), p. 300.

American marriage—the work of Paul Jacobson— reveals
the early American rate of permanent bachelorhood to
have been a steadily rising one that peaked during the
lifetimes of the men born around 1865-1870 (i.e., men
just entering their adulthood in the late 1880s and early
1890s). Jacobson's cohort analyses of bachelors and
spinsters (single whites aged 15 and over) from succes-
sive decades of the late eighteenth century through the
nineteenth century show that

> there was a gradual decrease in the proportion
> ultimately marrying among persons born in successive
> periods up to the years immediately after the Civil
> War, and thereafter a gradual increase.

Jacobson notes further that

> the marriage rate for bachelors and spinsters has
> generally moved upward during this century. Among
> single men, for example, the average annual marriage
> rate rose from 64 per 1,000 in the 1900s to 69 in the
> 1920s. Although the rate dropped sharply during the
> depression of the 1930s, it soared upward in the next
> decade to the unusually high level of 92 per 1,000.
>
> Another indication of the increased propensity to
> marry is afforded by the extent to which the single
> population has been depleted. Among males aged 15
> and over (including those in the armed forces
> overseas) the proportion single declined from 42
> percent in 1890 ... to less than 25 per cent in
> 1950.[39]

---

[39] Paul Jacobson, *American Marriage and Divorce* (New York:
Rinehart, 1959), p. 35. For additional details, see especially
Tables 7 and 8, pp. 34-35. The paragraphs above assess fully
neither the heterosexual bachelor subculture nor its former place
in American life, but attempt merely to indicate that such
assessment is a desideratum in American historiography.

Not only were there more lifelong bachelors earlier, but there were more "bachelor years" for men who eventually married (the average age at marriage was greater).

Toward the middle of the nineteenth century, hard upon the great waves of Irish and German immigration, the American poolroom began to emerge as the major physical locus of the rising bachelor subculture. One witness to the start of the boom wrote as follows in 1850:

> The rapidity with which Billiard rooms have increased in this and other cities of the Union, is extraordinary. Within the writer's memory, the number of rooms in New York, did not exceed seven or eight, and perhaps not more than sixteen tables in all; now, there are from fifty to sixty rooms, with a number of tables, varying from one to sixteen each, and amounting, on the whole, to something over four hundred.[40]

The periodical of the time most concerned with "popular culture," *Frank Leslie's Illustrated Newspaper*, in January 1859 began a regular column on billiards. April of the same year saw the first thing approximating a national championship contest, the Phelan-Seereiter match in Detroit.[41] The popularity that the sport had

---

[40] Michael Phelan, *Billiards Without a Master* (New York: D. D. Winant, 1850), p. 122. This, the first American book on billiards, went into several editions. Phelan also issued the first American billiard periodical, *Billiard Cue*, from 1856 to 1874; it was a monthly of four folio pages. Cf. Frank Luther Mott, *A History of American Magazines 1850-1865* (Cambridge, Mass.: Harvard University Press, 1938), p. 203.

[41] The names of the contestants are significant. In keeping with ethnic shifts in American immigration, most of the early non-WASP billiard professionals are of Irish origin (Phelan, Daly,

already gained is indicated by the fact that this match, the first professional billiard event for which admission was charged, was a sellout at the high admission price of $5, was played for the enormous prize of $15,000 (surely over $100,000 in today's currency), and was altogether one of the most gripping events on the American "sporting imagination" of the nineteenth century. *The New York Times'* coverage of the match— —this when the whole newspaper was only eight to twelve pages—appears in several columns over three separate issues. In 1865 the periodical *Round Table* took note of "the mania for playing billiards which has developed itself in this country in the last five or six years."[42]

The swift increase noted at mid-century was a mere beginning. The pace of poolroom growth accelerated throughout the second half of the nineteenth century and well into the twentieth. By the mid-1920s America

---

Kavanagh, Gallagher, Keogh, McKenna, *et al.*) or of German origin (Seereiter, Schaefer, Kieckhefer, Reiselt, Hoppe, *et al.*), with Italians and Jews becoming prominent in the picture only after the turn of the century.

The heavy extent to which German-Americans were involved in billiards has been overlooked by billiard historians, probably because the first American billiard books were written by Irishmen, but there is much evidence apart from the names of early professionals. For example, in the middle of the nineteenth century a number of the German beer gardens along the Bowery in New York City had billiard tables. Cf. Matthew Hale Smith, *Sunshine and Shadow in New York* (Hartford, Conn.: J. B. Burr, 1869), p. 216. For an amusing sidelight on German-American billiard playing, cf. Max Weber, "The Protestant Sects and the Spirit of Capitalism," in H. H. Gerth and C. Wright Mills, eds., *From Max Weber: Essays in Sociology* (New York: Galaxy Books, Oxford University Press, 1958), pp. 310-311.

[42] Quoted in Mott, *op. cit.,* p. 203.

had over 42,000 poolrooms (over 4,000 in New York City alone), many with more than 50 tables each and even a few with 100 tables each.[43] Detroit Recreation, a poolroom in Detroit that claimed to be the world's largest, had 125 tables. In the 1920s, Ralph Greenleaf, the greatest pool champion in the history of the game, played the Palace Theatre at a salary of $2,000 per week. And note what happened to one of the instruction manuals, *Daly's Billiard Book*, which was published in 1913: in its first ten years, it achieved a larger sale than any other book devoted to a physical sport or game that had ever been published.[44]

The timing of all this is significant beyond the fact of

---

[43] Statistics on the number of poolrooms, put out from time to time by such organizations as the Billiard Congress of America, National Billiard Council, and Billiard Room Proprietors Association of America, vary considerably. The consensus seems to be that in 1964 there were 11,000 poolrooms, up more than 3,000 from 1960. Estimates of the peak number of poolrooms in the 1920s vary between 40,000 and 45,000, with 42,000 the most frequently used figure. Estimates of the peak number of poolrooms in New York City in the 1920s range from 4,000 to 5,000; according to reporter Robert Deasy (*World Telegram & Sun*, June 24, 1963), in 1961 New York City had only 257 licensed poolrooms with a total of 2,177 tables and in 1962 (after the revival had begun) had 291 poolrooms with 2,504 tables. According to Dixie Dean Harris (*Pageant*, August, 1964, p. 114), Detroit had a thousand poolrooms in the 1920s but only 156 poolrooms in 1964. Robert Coughlan (*op. cit.*, p. 166) estimates that the number of pool and billiard tables in use had declined from over 500,000 in the 1920s to only one-fifth that number in 1951. Although these and other published statistics permit of no exact agreement, the enormous magnitude of the decline from the 1920s is clear enough in all of them.

[44] .Cf. Maurice Daly, *Daly's Billiard Book*, 6th ed. (Chicago: A. C. McClurg & Co., 1923), p. [viii].

bachelorhood *per se*. It is not accidental that poolrooms began rapidly to increase in number and size as the American frontier rapidly receded, for one function of the frontier was as a male escape-hatch from effete and "feminized" urban civilization.[45] As towns and cities spread ever westward and as they more and more "settled down," the poolroom blossomed as a kind of behind-the-lines or inner frontier, the new no-woman's land, catering to internal refugees from the world of female-imposed gentility, catering to men who wanted to be able to curse and spit tobacco, fight freely, dress sloppily, gamble heavily, get roaring drunk, whore around.

Nor is it accidental that Mark Twain, the American author we most associate with chafing at his entrapment in the respectability of urban civilization and with nostalgic longing for woman-free frontier days, should of all American authors be the one most truly to fall in love with billiard playing and poolroom life.[46] Nor is it accidental that the poolroom and the heterosexual bachelor disappear simultaneously from the American

---

[45] Awareness of this role of the frontier runs through much of early American literature; cf. Leslie Fielder, *Love and Death in the American Novel* (New York: Criterion Books, 1960), *passim.*
[46] Cf. William Dean Howells, "My Memories of Mark Twain," *Harper's Monthly Magazine,* Vol. 121 (July 1910), pp. 170-71; Albert Bigelow Paine, *Mark Twain: A Biography* (New York: Harper and Brothers, 1912), Vol. 2, pp. 613-14, and Vol. 3, pp. 1324-32, 1366-70; Willie Hoppe, *Thirty Years of Billiards* (New York: G. P. Putnam's, 1925), pp. 109-114, 117. According to Hoppe, Twain attended every big billiard match in New York for years. From Paine's account, especially pp. 613-14, it appears that Twain used his own billiard playing as a means of getting together with male cronies to the exclusion of his wife and daughter.

landscape (which is why not the Depression, but the easing of the Depression was the real death-knell of the poolroom). Nor is it accidental that the most regular and devoted of today's poolroom spectators, the old men who come day after day and use the poolroom as a poor man's club, consist overwhelmingly of old-style bachelors and once-bitten-twice-shy widowers. Nor, finally, is it accidental that the most regular and devoted of today's poolroom players, the pool and billiard hustlers who virtually live in the poolroom and build their very careers around poolroom life, comprise one of the last American occupational groups in which the majority of adults are nonhomosexual bachelors.

As Friedrich Nietzsche first observed, an institution when deprived of its major function does not *eo ipso* go out of business, but often survives and prospers by taking on new functions.[47] Modern sociology, with its studies of the changing role of the family, the church, the settlement house, etc., has abundantly confirmed Nietzsche's insight. Might not the poolroom in this way flourish once more—by redefining itself as a place "for the family" and catering to women as well as men, as indeed most new-look poolrooms are trying to do? In theory, yes; in practice, no. An institution that tries to change its function sometimes fails, and this appears to be the poolroom's fate. Of course, poolrooms will not cease to exist, and their number may even increase a bit over the next few years, but there are several reasons why "cleaning up the game" and changing its "image" so as to attract women will never restore to poolrooms

---

[47]Cf. Section XII of " 'Guilt,' 'Bad Conscience,' and the Like," *Genealogy of Morals.*

anything remotely like the degree of popularity they once had.

Bringing women in—with the attendant paraphernalia of free instruction for them, special women's tournaments, the curbing of obscenity and other loutish male behavior so that women will feel comfortable, etc.—has been tried several times before.[48] Each time it has had a modicum of initial success and then died. This is only to be expected.

Granted three notable exceptions—the billiard player May Kaarlus around the turn of the century, the pool player Ruth McGinnis in the 1930s, and the billiard player Masako Katsura today—poolroom games pose near-insuperable problems for women. First, male-female differences in the structure of the arm affect development of a good stroke, making it very difficult for a woman to become good at these games relative to other games (just as a woman can, if she is athletically adept, become a good bowler or underhand softball pitcher but can never learn to throw a ball overhand very well). Secondly, many shots require leaning way over the table or even putting one leg up on the table, involving a display of legs (if a skirt is worn) or buttocks (if slacks are worn) that most women find quite embarrassing. Thirdly and most importantly, there are the kind of teenage boys and men who hang around poolrooms. No poolroom proprietor can completely curb their profanity, leering, attempts to pick up the women. Nor can he really get rid of them, for the simple

---

[48]For example, see *Billiards Magazine* (June, 1932), pp. 6-9. See also "Swank Pool Hall Attracts Women of Springfield, Ill.," *Life,* Vol. 23 (November 17, 1947), pp. 71-72; the poolroom described in this article later went out of business.

reason that they represent the great bulk of his business.

That last point is crucial. For nearly all the women who play, it is a passing fad, something that lately *Mademoiselle* and *Vogue* and even *Saturday Evening Post* have told them is "in" but that is forgotten when the next new kick comes along. For the reasons just stated, women almost never stick with poolroom games; they soon tend to visit the poolroom infrequently or drop out completely, whereas the men are far more likely to be or become regular players.[49] And the new-style poolrooms hopeful of catering to women are quickly finding this out. Once the initial novelty has

---

[49] Private (nonpoolroom) playing by the upper class, which I have not tried to discuss in detail in this study, shows a different pattern of female participation. Although women were of course excluded from playing at men's clubs, the attitude toward their playing at home varied at different times and places; sometimes the home billiard room was an exclusively male preserve, but usually women were also allowed to play, and often did so. Thus Robert Kerr advised that the home billiard room should "be situated not exactly amongst the Dwelling-rooms, but still in close connection with them, for the access of the ladies" (Kerr, *op. cit.,* 3rd ed., p. 120). Women playing billiards at home are shown in many British and American engravings of the eighteenth and nineteenth centuries, e.g., in Rowlandson's "The Billiard Table" (1820) from his *Dr. Syntax* series. This tradition of upper-class female billiard playing has few exemplars today, the most notable being the Queen Mother of England.

On the other hand, since *The Hustler* America has witnessed a spectacular rise in playing at home by the upper-middle class (as evidenced by the continuing boom in sales of small-sized tables to homeowners). Thus, despite the shaky prospects of today's poolrooms, pool *playing* might yet become almost as popular as it once was—but as a home activity rather than a public one. New York's most experienced billiard table mechanic, Robert Cappelli, informs me that today over three-fourths of his installation jobs are for tables in suburban homes.

worn off, the proprietor finds that his trade consists mostly of teenage boys, especially the school dropouts, and secondarily the old-style "sporting" types among the adult males. They play so much oftener and longer than women or teenage girls that he can't afford to kick them out.

Many of the new poolrooms are doing good business, notably those in postwar population centers that never had poolrooms before. The revival has indeed found enough of a market to support such places. But already the cream has been skimmed off this market. Already a number of poolrooms that opened with the fanciest of intentions now must rely on clientele who are anything but fancy; for example, one suburban poolroom that two years ago received acres of publicity about its "respectability" is now a center of narcotics distribution. Already, in every section of the country, the rate at which new poolrooms are opening is going down. Already many of the snazzy new poolrooms are in financial trouble, falling behind in their payments to the equipment manufacturers. Already, as some fall so far behind that their creditors will no longer carry them, the bankruptcy rate is rising sharply. And that's with only about a fourth as many poolrooms as America had when its population was little over half what it is now. The heyday of the poolroom is over.

Why People Play Poker

THOMAS M. MARTINEZ and ROBERT LaFRANCHI

More Americans play poker than any other card game. They also win (and lose) more money at poker than at any other card game. And, as has often been remarked, poker is somehow quintessentially American. Marshall McLuhan considers the game to be "the expression of all the complex attitudes and unspoken values of a competitive society," calling for "shrewdness, aggression, trickery, and unflattering appraisals of character." Be that as it may, most experts agree that poker demands enormous skill and science from the winning player.

Probability theory predicts that in the long run every good player will hold the same amount of good, bad and indifferent hands. That being the case, the basic difference between the skilled and the unskilled player is that the former will have the patience to wait out a run of bad cards by betting cautiously, while the poor player will bet on all the indifferent and some of the bad hands so recklessly that by the time his luck turns, the possibility of recouping his losses is almost hopeless.

That may sound like a simple enough prescription for success, but the difficulty is that not many people can stand the pressure of losing money while waiting for winning cards. Of the estimated 300 people whom we observed over the course of four years at a commercial card parlor in California, *only 10 players* were able to take the strain of periodic losing streaks and emerge in the long run as consistent winners. All 10 gambled according to the same plan of bringing to bear the maximum patience and self-control.

Very simply, the good poker player is one who has learned when and how much to bet on a winning hand; but he also knows when and how to bluff his opponents. There is a good deal of misunderstanding about bluffing, however, which is why we'd like to touch on it first.

For most people, bluffing is the act of pretending that you have better cards in your hand than you really have. This is only one kind of bluffing, though, and it's interesting to note that the people who believe they can win pots of money that way are almost always the losers, or those who don't know anything about the science of the game at all.

It is widely believed that poker players are good psychologists and are especially adept at reading their opponents' gestures. This is true; many good players do find it useful to attempt to "psyche out" the others around the table. Nevertheless, it is our impression (an impression buttressed by conversations with some of the best players we have known) that the ability to analyze one's opponents is distinctly secondary to those qualities of self-control and patience we mentioned earlier.

Still, a good deal of bluffing goes on, and among the subtler forms, two of the most common are the reverse and the double reverse. Pat, for example, is taking longer than usual to make his bet. He is trying to signal something to his opponents, namely that he cannot make up his mind because his cards are only minimally decent. Meanwhile, Mike is unobtrusively (i.e. with that well-known "poker face") observing Pat's behavior. He realizes that Pat is trying to represent himself as having a poor hand. Pat is indeed so trying to represent himself, but Mike, if he is like the majority of poker players, will persist in believing the opposite of what he thinks the other player is trying to signal to him. This is called using reverse psychology.

The player who uses the double-reverse strategy will try to signal something about his hand, hoping however that the other players will think the opposite. The best clue as to whether a person is using a reverse or a double-reverse strategy is that with the latter he will make a very deliberate, highly visible move, such as throwing his chips at the pot. His hope is that the next time he makes a similar gesture the other players will recall his earlier move and associate it with his hand at that time. It is more often the good players who use this strategy, but they don't do it very often. Poor players, who bluff more anyway, tend to use the double reverse to the point that anyone could see through it.

The type of game influences the bluffing strategy of the good player. In a "low-limit" game, it does not pay to advertise, that is, to lead people to think you have better cards than you do. This is because the size of the pot almost guarantees that the bluff will be called. In games with very high or no limits on the stakes, the bluff becomes a very significant factor. Here it does pay to advertise. Early in a game, for example, a good player might be content to make a bluff and have it called. This is known as creating a "tell," which he can use later in the game to suggest a bluff, except that this time he really will have high cards.

It is extremely difficult not to become self-conscious when one is dealt a good hand. Good players repress this, however, as well as any demonstration of confidence. The reason is that the obviously confident player—when he has reason to be—runs three greater risks than are normally desirable. First, if he has a run of good luck, his demeanor will become predictable and he will lose any advantage that could be gained from bluffing. Second, the other players might simply call his bets without raising, thus cutting down on his winnings. And third, if he loses the hand, he also loses more face than would have been the case if he hadn't appeared so confident.

Probably the best type of psychological strategy is to adopt what is known as a "tight-player mystique." This means creating the appearance of one who rigidly follows a rational plan throughout the game, patiently waiting for winning cards, carefully controlling his bets. When a player is perceived as a rational, cautious person, he is in a much better position to use any of the forms of bluffing, for credibility is part of the impression he will have created. By the same token, in contrast to the player overly confident of his cards, the tight player gives the impression of being confident of himself, which is much more disheartening to one's opponents.

Needless to say, an enormous amount of tension often builds up around the poker table and it has to find outlets in forms of expression that don't themselves contribute to heighten the tensions and thus disrupt the game. In fact, we found that an important distinction between good and poor losers, and good and poor winners, was whether their actions tended to provoke or reduce the amount of tension in the game. Thus, for example, when the good winner attributes his success to luck, he has given the loser an opportunity to blame his loss on bad luck. The bad winner, on the other hand, attributes his success to his skill and may even needle the losers. Another type of bad winner, though, is someone who talks incessantly, always apologizes for winning, or recalls his past losses while raking in the pot. Gamblers tend to reinforce their own and others' conformity to acceptable modes of behavior by making continual references to individual players who typify the outer limits of permissible behavior. In some instances, one individual serves as a model for two types of behavior. We found several players who have the reputation of being both good winners and good losers and are considered "perfect gentlemen to play cards with."

There is an important qualification, however, with respect to the amount of "poor sportsmanship" that gamblers will tolerate in a loser. Naturally, the game couldn't go on for very long if losing players were permitted to curse the winners, throw their cards at the dealer, or upset the table; but a certain amount of abuse is tolerated by winners. How much, as a general rule, is directly related to the offender's "action," that is, the amount of money he loses and how fast. Winning is its own compensation; from the loser a certain amount of bad feeling is acceptable, if only to keep the fellow in the game . . . to lose some more.

To attract as many customers as possible, the house

tries to run a quiet, relaxed game with plenty of fast action. To achieve this, the management subtly tries to enforce the model behavior of good winners and good losers. Much depends, in this effort, on the dealer's ability to spot behavior that might possibly result in friction with other players. In that event, the dealer usually adopts an intermediary, conciliatory stance in order to prevent the development of further trouble. If, for example, a winner says to one of the losers, "You played that hand badly," the dealer must quickly determine how the loser will react. If he sees that an argument is coming, the dealer might immediately cut in to get the players involved in the next hand, saying, "Well, gentlemen, another hand, another winner." If an argument does break out, the dealer advises the manager, who confers privately with the offending player, seeking to get him to respect the other players and the game rules. If repeated interventions of this kind fail, the offending player will be barred.

In addition to dealing, making change, and verifying bets, the dealer's other duties include enforcing the mechanical rules of the game, and serving as a sort of sponge to absorb the frustrations of the losers. Since the dealers are working on a percentage basis, they are actually working for the players. The more the players are pleased with the game, the more they will come back and the more money the dealers will make. This situation creates a certain amount of conflict for the dealers, because they are also, of course, working for the manager, whose orders are to strictly enforce all the mechanical rules. In doing so, however, the dealer is likely to offend some players. Although other players may also get angry if the rules are not strictly enforced, the dealer usually resolves his conflict-of-interest by being somewhat lax in enforcing the rules, since, on the whole, players are not as interested as the manager in strict enforcement.

As mentioned earlier, the manners of good winning and good losing call for losses to be blamed on bad luck. The manager and dealers assiduously promote this practice to "cool out" the losers, even though it means that the dealer himself becomes the ultimate target of the loser's rage. Since he deals the cards, enforces the rules, and acts as mediator, he is the visible representation of the luck of the game. Sometimes heavy losers hurl insults at the dealers and, although the manager does not condone such behavior, again it is tolerated because the heavy losers "make" the game. In turn, the dealers often try to release the tension created by the abuse they get by making some such crack as "When the players win, they're skillful; when they lose, it's a lousy dealer."

The single factor that appears most important in understanding the behavior of poker players is their relationship and attitude toward winning and losing. In this regard, we found it useful to distinguish four types of players. First, there are the consistent winners. Second, there are the break-evens, whose wins and losses tend to cancel out over a year's play. Third, are the losers, those who try to win but consistently lose. Finally, there are the action players, those who compulsively try to lose.

Because of the fast action of the game, and because every player wins and loses at some point or other, we were able to see how each of these four types of players reacted to the outcome of the cards. We found that consistent winners generally exhibited all the traits expected of the model "good" winner, and so, to a lesser extent, did those who broke even. Not surprisingly, the behavior of the losers and action players, regardless of whether they actually won or lost a particular hand, tended to raise the level of tension. As one player put it, however, "It's easy for John to be a good loser, he wins most of the time."

The difference between a loser and an action player is that the latter, in the eyes of the other players, seems to want to lose his money. He is not stupid, but he bets in the most uncontrolled way and his bluffs are utterly transparent. He plays poor hands, worse even than those of the losers. In lowball poker, the game we observed most often, the player with the lowest cards wins. The science of the game is that a one-card draw or a pat hand is the only really playable hand. In a game of six or seven good players, hands are seldom opened. A poor player, however, when dealt a 6, a 4 and a 2 to begin with, would perhaps draw two more cards. The action player with that hand would not only open, he would probably raise with it, in an attempt to bluff the other players out of the pot.

The action player most resembles the popular and literary stereotype of the compulsive gambler. Yet he is also the "deviant" in commercial poker playing. Statistically, he represents only about 2 percent of the regular players. Others do not seem to understand him. Many think he is crazy because he plays recklessly a game that they take seriously. They cannot even put themselves into his shoes, for most players are unable to develop enough momentum to detach themselves from the value they place on the symbolic meanings of the poker game. Yet, none of the other players really wants the action player to become like the rest of them, and lose his lucrative contribution. The action player is not considered a sucker, however; his money is lost in free, open competition.

The action player follows the formal rules of the game, but his plunging luck-reliant betting demonstrates to others that reckless playing will always lose in the end. Luck is too whimsical to depend upon it too much. But no one really thinks the action player is just unlucky, because no reasonable player expects luck to compensate for careless betting. His playing behavior provides a useful contrast; it highlights the importance of rational, patient control over betting as the superior guide for winning.

The action player's continual violation of the informal rules of the game, mostly engaging in bad-loser behavior, strengthens the general rule that tolerance for another player's game behavior is directly related to his action. Only an action player can complain so loudly about losing and get away with it. A loser comes to understand that he cannot complain as much as the action player unless he loses as much, which he usually does not. In addition, the loser does not want to be regarded as he regards the action player, as somewhat of a farce. In this sense, the deviant (action player) helps to define by example the tolerable range of acceptable behavior for the overwhelming majority of players.

Even the action player himself does not seem to want (or need) to blame his losses on bad luck. When other players, especially winners and break-evens, chalk up the action player's losing to bad luck, they are not saying it to keep his self-esteem intact, but to cut short a particularly vociferous outburst of bad-loser behavior. Unlike the consistent loser, who feels relieved of the personal responsibility for losing when he is told to blame his luck, the action player calms down temporarily upon hearing similar words because he senses that he has complained loudly enough already, and that any more might lead the other players to pressures, which will be explained more fully later.

Since the action player does not want to give the impression that he cannot handle his job, he aims the bulk of his complaints toward the card game. He knows that other players will tolerate more violations of the usual informal rules if he is willing to lose a large amount of money in the game. If he wants to be granted privileges, he has to pay the price.

The action player's strategy of playing according to the informal rules serves another function for him. In his mind, betting recklessly will influence other players to see him as a financial success in his work—someone to whom losing money means almost nothing, someone worthy of their respect and admiration. He enjoys complaining about his losses, but he also wants to convey the impression that it is just a game to him, one that he does not take as seriously as the other players. He thinks that the other players tolerate his griping because they secretly admire and respect him, and thus grant him the special privileges of an elite person in their midst. Unbeknownst to him is the sad fact that the other players do not care about what he may be or earn outside the cardroom; he is someone to be laughed at when he is not around, but highly valued when he is.

Some losers become like action players in the course of a game. After losing about $100, they begin to get nervous and start gambling more recklessly. Losers also tend to drink more than the others, perhaps to calm their nerves. The more they lose, the more they drink, and the more they play like the action players. Action players themselves, however, always play in the same fashion whether they drink or not.

When the average player finds himself acting like a bad loser, he often knows it is time to quit playing for a while, because such behavior is associated with a consistent loser. A player with sufficient insight realizes the importance of detachment and coolness to winning. Quite often, he will get up to "cool off" for a few minutes, and then return after getting back into the frame of mind that will help him resist the pressure of losing until he gets a good run of cards. Winners do this the most, next are the break-evens, then losers, and action players not at all. Action players do not care about keeping cool, in fact they do not want any part of it while they play. Winners seldom blow their cool. Losers often blow what little they had at the beginning, and are later sometimes reminded that perhaps they should try to simmer down so that they do not disrupt the game. Other losers come to recognize bad-loser behavior as detrimental to their playing and voluntarily try to cool themselves down. It is this growing ability to recognize one's behavior in response to losing and winning that is a transitional stage between a consistent loser and a break-even. Few consistent losers, however, ever develop this ability to see that it is their reaction to losing that causes them to continue to lose.

Losers also tend to attach the most importance to the merit and status that comes from winning in poker. One heavy loser, for example, told us privately, "I can't seem to win at lowball. I win at other games and I've done well at my jobs, but I can't seem to beat this one. I try to play well, but my luck's so bad I can't win. If I could only beat this game. . . ." This player, we discovered, had tried and failed at several managerial positions in the field of service and sales promotion, failures that were generally attributed by others to his unfriendly nature. We also found that he had never won at gambling and that his greater losses at lowball were probably due to the greater demands made upon his patience by the faster action. Perhaps he lied about his past winnings to acquire the image of a successful gambler. And since he recurrently failed at securing managerial status, his gambling could also be seen as an effort to support a sagging self-image. If he had finished his last sentence with insight, it might have gone like this: "If I could only beat this game, then I would have proved to the world and to myself that I have what it takes."

The meaning of "luck" varies with different types of poker players. To winners and break-evens, luck is less than half the game, and not enough to count on to win consistently. As one winner put it, "It's what one does with his luck that counts." These two types of players do not depend upon the opinions of other players to bolster their self-esteem, since they know that the admiration of losers is always silent. Winning the pot is sufficient indication of their worth as poker players.

The consistent loser thinks he might win, if he gets the right luck. His perception of the statistical probability of holding winning cards is distorted by his great desire to win and his heavy reliance upon luck, rather than upon skill. The meaning of luck to the loser is twofold. On the one hand, he believes luck is what makes one player a winner and another a loser. With such a view, the loser can save face even as he loses, for his fate is out of his control—"lady luck did it." On the other hand, he wants to regard himself as having the ability to play well and, of course, to win consistently. When he does win, he wants to define it as a victory of his personal skill over luck. This is a major reason the loser is often a bad winner, proclaiming that his skill is what did it. The action player is not concerned with luck in the poker game. When he does win, he usually considers himself lucky; seldom does he seriously think he has a good chance of winning the way he plays. Others do not evaluate the action player in terms normally applied to most players because he does not play for real.

Poker is a game in which a person's ideas about himself are often influenced and shaped, much as in everyday life, and in society. We all want to be defined as winners. It is probably a safe assumption that the same people who blame their gambling losses on bad luck rather than lack of skill will also blame bad luck for their other failures. The poker game, however, more easily accommodates this view of the world, because the winners tolerate and reinforce it in order to secure the loser's money. The losers will more readily go on playing if they can console themselves by blaming their bad luck. We often heard an angry loser effectively quieted down by just four words from another player or the dealer, "You really are unlucky."

In the same sense that losers find some comfort in blaming their losses on bad luck, a secure, favorable self-image is associated with winning. A consistent winner may publicly attribute his winnings to good luck in order to reduce game tension and not make the losers feel too bad, but privately he knows it is his skill, not good luck, that makes him a winner.

The development of the consistent winner's self-image is seen in the case of Joe. His lowball winnings are phenomenal, due mainly to his prodigious patience. He remains calm while losing large amounts of money, confidently waiting for his run of good cards and for the other players to make mistakes. Even the other winning players are amazed at Joe's cool. But there appears to be a logical explanation for his behavior. Joe, a likeable fellow who does not mind good-natured kidding, caught on to the game of lowball at the outset of his cardplaying career about five years ago, and he began winning small amounts of money. The other players, dealers, and the proprietor started teasing him with remarks such as, "Hey, champ, you sure can play this game!" As his winnings increased, the teasing increased. Recently, one of the more perceptive players finally started denouncing the teasing and pointed out, "You shouldn't tell him how good he is. He believes you and it helps his play." By now, however, it is too late. Joe is a consistent winner, regardless of how much pressure is put on his patience by both other players and runs of poor cards. In Joe's case, the self-image of a successful gambler, calm and patient, was apparently created by the others in the give-and-take of the game itself.

In order to obtain some understanding of the characteristics of each type of poker player away from the table and to relate these characteristics to their gambling behavior, we selected a representative sample of 60 players who came in during a year's time. Since the cardroom is not easily amenable to standard interviewing techniques, our method of gathering data was through casual conversation and necessarily limited.

All of the players were men, most of whom were middle-aged, married and high-school graduates with steady jobs. This finding disputes the popular image of card parlors as homes for transients and the criminally inclined. Although personal-income data were not obtained, the players' occupations reveal that most of them were in the lower-middle income bracket.

In general, the winners were single or divorced, in contrast to an overwhelming majority of the other players who were married. They were also slightly younger than most players. Those who broke even tended to be white-collar workers who played poker twice a week. In other social characteristics such as age, education or marital status, they resembled the average poker player one might find in a card parlor. The losers tended to be somewhat less-educated than most other players, and, perhaps more important, as a group they had the lowest occupational status. The outstanding characteristic of the action players was their occupation; all of whom we observed were small-business men. They also tended to be slightly older than most players.

The desire to gamble, as expressed in frequency of playing, appears to be higher for both winners and losers.

A common characteristic of the losers, which helps explain their nervous reaction to losing, is that they are usually gambling with money they can scarcely afford to lose. They may also be trying, more than the others, to earn the status of success. Action players, on the other hand, do not get nervous about losing, although they complain about it. One reason for this is that the action players are playing with money they can afford to lose.

In addition to the objective social characteristics of poker players, we also probed the subjective meanings that the players attached to other aspects of their lives. In particular, we were interested in the meanings they attached to their job, friends and leisure.

We found that action players were the least satisfied with their jobs. Even in the midst of a game, they would often complain about the demands made on them by their business and customers. Forced to keep their emotions in check during work, action players apparently used poker to give vent to built-up tensions. Since, as big losers, their game behavior was tolerated to the point where they felt free to let off almost as much steam as they cared to, poker for the action player is sort of a therapy, a release.

The losers appear to be social isolates; poker is their main interest. Neither job, nor friends, nor leisure activities and hobbies are as meaningful to the loser as is poker. One hears them, usually when they are gambling most furiously, complaining about arguments with their wives or bosses, or making "philosophical" statements about the proper role of husband and wife. This suggests that, for losers, poker is sought as a form of compensation or escape from anomic social relations.

Those who break even are more satisfied with their job than either losers or action players, and they usually complain much less about work or marital problems. Perhaps this relative freedom from home and job problems allows them to concentrate on the science of the poker game and the smooth flow of hands.

Winners are outgoing, gregarious people, with an air of not having a care in the world. They like their job, have plenty of friends, and are involved in many different activities, from golfing to fishing to betting on the horses. For the winners, poker is neither a release nor an escape, but a way of life, a continuation of a game they thoroughly enjoy and master.

Freud once theorized that gambling was an unconscious substitute for masturbation. We find it more useful, however, to try to understand why people play poker by exploring the symbolic meanings of player interaction and the social characteristics of the players. If poker playing is a substitute for other things in life, they are likely to be social and not necessarily sexual satisfactions that are being substituted for.

We are suggesting that those who are on the periphery of social life, the losers, seem to use gambling as a substitute for satisfactory primary relationships. For action players, a poker game is a social situation that allows a release of tension, something that is not provided by their normal social activities.

Winners and those who break even, both of whom usually have satisfactory social relationships, appear to play poker for reasons somewhat different from losers and action players. They seem to play primarily for the satisfaction of succeeding through personal skill. Winners and break-evens also enjoy the gamesmanship of being the good winner and good loser; under this kind of stress, they pride themselves on keeping their "cool." At poker they have a fateful situation for highlighting and reinforcing this much-admired quality.

While private poker playing, the weekly game with the boys, is not quite the same as a commercial game, many of the symbolic meanings of player interaction as discussed here are likely to apply. There is also a good chance that many of the players will attach meanings to the game similar to the ones we analyzed.

Originally, we were interested in finding out why and how people would continually lose in a game of skill. Why didn't they learn how to win? We found that for consistent losers, whether compulsive or not, other meanings are attached to poker playing, meanings that are often so potent that they overwhelm the desire to develop the skills to win.

In short, why and how one plays poker is influenced by one's outlook toward and satisfaction with life in general, including wife, job, friends and leisure. Further, one's relationship to the game as a winner or loser, good sport or bad sport is more or less an extension of meanings one seeks to maintain, or compensate for, in our society: increasingly risk-free, impersonal and driving toward achievement.

A NOTE ON METHODOLOGY

One of us (LaFranchi) had already been working for two years as a dealer and part-time manager in a commercial cardroom at the time we met. After discovering our mutual interests, we began working together for the next two years, structuring our conversations and engaging in extensive conversations with the other players.

While the bulk of the information and all of the statistics were obtained inside one commercial cardroom, we played at other card parlors in order to gain further insights into why and how people play poker.

We cannot describe in detail the cardroom in which we spent most of our research time, because we want to protect the anonymity of the players and don't want to endanger our future research. However, most commercial cardrooms in Northern California are located near downtown districts and are well-kept, clean business establishments, often operated in conjunction with a bar. The number of tables varies from 3 to 15, the average being about 6 tables. While not as ornate or as noisy as most Nevada casinos, these cardrooms are not as barren as most poolrooms, nor as quiet.

July/August 1969

FURTHER READING
The Psychology of Gambling by Edmund Bergler (New York: Hill

and Wang, 1957) provides a psychological approach to gambling behavior and analysis of gamblers.

Scarne's Complete Guide to Gambling by John Scarne (New York: Simon and Schuster, 1961) is a comprehensive description of the "ins" and "outs" of almost every form of gambling, with some interesting facts of the history of different games of chance.

The Racing Game by Marvin B. Scott (Chicago: Aldine, 1968) is an insightful and sociological case study of a major form of gambling (horse racing). Scott views gambling as a problem in the organization of information.

Making vs. Playing Games of Cards

E. LOUIS MAHIGEL and GREGORY P. STONE

Consider the schoolboy football player, the girl on the barstool, the black man on the streetcorner, the white man in the Brooks Brothers suit, or the poker player anywhere. They have something in common, which is that all can be called hustlers with varying degrees of praise or blame, depending on who is doing the labelling and who is being labelled.

We like this moral ambiguity in the word hustler; it is just what is needed for our subjects, gamblers, in that it merely connotes their status as men who happen to derive a substantial amount of their income from playing cards. To say of a gambler that he is a hustler says little about how he plays cards except that he probably plays very well. It certainly doesn't mean that he cheats, either all of the time or only when he can. Cheaters are hustlers who use illegitimate techniques.

But not all hustlers are cheaters, even though they are thoroughly familiar with most, if not all, the cheaters' techniques.

There is another useful connotation of the word hustler. It points to a conscious manipulation of people and things in the field of play—football, sex, survival, advertising or gambling—to the end of winning. Social scientists have used various phrases to describe this practice: Ralph Turner has called it role making; Erving Goffman has called it staging or impression management; especially useful is Anselm Strauss' concept of status forcing. These terms place different emphases on different aspects of the situation, but taken together they all remind us that a game is not just played. It can also be made.

Making the game of cards is more than giving them a riffle or a cut, although for most card players, even those who play for serious stakes, that about sums it up. We know that playing cards for money is widespread in this country. Yet there are literally millions of players in every segment of the population who are content to shuffle a deck, cut or decline to cut, and deal or await the deal. They scarcely conceive that making the cards frequently involves for those who financially depend upon gambling a whole range of techniques that have had to be mastered with care and skill.

Of course, the hustler may not use all the techniques we will discuss here. His mere knowledge of the game (hands, pots, bluffs, odds and reading an opponent's style of play) gives him a 10 to 25 percent edge in, for example, any poker game. Cheaters, naturally, break the rules in many ways, as we shall see. But in some games cheating may not be possible, and so the cheater may be obliged to hustle legitimately at times. But, for now, let us look at some of the techniques available to him if he does cheat.

Gimmicks, like most equipment used in any industry, are produced in "factories." As used by the gambler, a factory refers to the production and distribution of cheating equipment under the same roof. As far as we know, the largest factory producing and distributing card equipment was once located in Chicago. This particular operation was closed in the early sixties but factories persist today throughout the world, in New York and London, of course, but also in Tulsa, Oklahoma, to name only three cities. Although these factories produce and distribute all kinds of gambling equipment such as dice, "put and take tops," table magnets and radio cue prompters, we will focus on the equipment produced for making the game of cards. Such gimmicks are only used by gamblers who cheat. Categories would include: 1) hold-out equipment, 2) stripped decks, 3) marked decks and 4) equipment to mark or "read" cards. All marking presupposes reading, but not all reading presupposes the use of marking equipment, for some gimmicks are manufactured to permit the reading of conventional cards. With the exception of hold-out equipment, these gimmicks are never mutually exclusive.

Hold-out Equipment are essentially containers. They are designed to facilitate palming or other ways of withdrawing, holding and reintroducing cards during the game. The simplest type is the table card-holder. This is a device that can be attached to the underside of a card table and hold any number of cards for easy retrieval. Only a rank amateur would use such a gimmick, because the skilled card cheat could use his leg, his arm pit or a jacket pocket to accomplish the same results, thereby minimizing the risk of detection. More subtle and complex equipment would include hold-out *machines*, elaborate metallic and vacuumatic devices concealed in the sleeve of the cheater and operated by arm pressure, knee movement or chest expansion. Like table card-holders, these machines enable the cheater to withdraw, hold and reintroduce cards during the course of the game, but they are more subtle because they are on the body of the gambler rather than attached to the props of the game, and bodies are more immune to scrutiny than the props are. Then too if the other players suspect the presence of a hold-out machine, the cheater can flee the scene with it if it's on his person, but the table card-holder, as with all other props, remains on the scene of action. Even so, both these types of devices are used very seldom, as the risks of detection are so great. On those rare occasions when a machine is used, the gambler must be extremely skilled, and the employment of such devices is dependent upon the naivete of the other players as well as the game that is being played. Even then the device is used infrequently. The master of this art is called a "machine man" in the trade.

Paper, Readers, and Reading. We have already said that it is impossible to separate writing from reading, so it is with making the game of cards. Marked cards (paper) are useless unless they can be read. Factories supply an incredible range of marked decks, for example, blockout work, brace work, line work, shade work and border work. One of the more popular techniques of marking cards is blocking out. Here a minor portion of the design on the back of the card is inked out, indicating to the cheater the value and sometimes the suit of the card. Brace work is an alteration of the design on the back of the card which conveys the value and/or suit of the card.

On the backs of most cards there are lines. Line work slightly expands these lines to indicate the cards that are in play, and cards so worked are important products of the factory. Shade work is accomplished by darkening a portion of the back of the card. Border work involves very slight alterations of the margin around the design on the back of a card. Sometimes this is called marked edge work and consists of providing minute bumps or bulges in various places around the margin of the design on the back of the card. The location of these bumps or bulges conveys to the skilled reader the value of the card but seldom, if ever, the suit.

At one time cards with a completely white back, devoid of design, were used, possibly as a safeguard against markings. Cheaters quickly got around this barrier by "waxing" or "glazing." Blank white backs of cards could be marked with minute smears of wax detectable only when the cards were held at odd angles. The cheater, of course, was extremely sensitized to the angle that would reveal the markings. We are tempted to say that methods of marking cards during play might well have begun as a reaction against efforts by gambling establishments to eliminate the marked deck, but we are not that naive.

All the above techniques for marking cards permit reading without special equipment. Yet, with the development of technology in the industry, more subtle methods for marking and reading cards have been developed, as, for example, luminous marks. These marks may only be used on red-backed cards, for the marking equipment is green, and, since red and green are primary colors which cancel one another out, the marks cannot be seen with the naked eye and reading them requires special equipment. This equipment once consisted of special spectacles or "shades," called luminous glasses and visors by those who are hip to the trade. Obviously, however, many card players know what rose colored spectacles are, so that they can only be used in making the game for rank fish or true suckers. Only unskilled cheaters would now consider using such reading equipment.

The development of contact lenses opened up new possibilities for reading luminous cards. Contacts can be discerned, of course, but only at a 90 degree angle from the side of the face and the cheater wearing contacts never presents this angle to the other players. Whether or not contact readers will be detected, therefore, is often a function of the skill and competence of the cheater. Cheaters must have poise, keeping the body always firmly in control, to make the game.

Equipment to Mark or "Read" Cards. Marking cards, as opposed to using marked decks, has probably been employed since the beginning of card playing. It has no documented history, like the greatest part of human conduct. Marking white backed cards with wax is a form of daubing, and this gimmick has been considerably elaborated upon and improved over the years. Not too long ago, the daub employed by the cheater had to match the color of the back of the deck but now technology has given the cheater "smoke" or "golden glow." This is a daub that can be applied to the back of almost any card regardless of its color. Daubs may be concealed in various places on the cheater's body—the hair, the moustache—or on clothing, for example, high-rimmed jacket buttons.

Cards can be marked in other ways as well. Sanding,

for example, means scratching the edge of cards without borders or margins. The cheater can produce his own devices for sanding, but the factories are in the business. Thus, "sand strips" are available on order from most factories. These are extremely small pieces of sandpaper which can be easily attached to the underside of the index or second finger, or, for that matter, whichever finger the gambler feels he can best use to mark cards.

For those cheaters who have an aversion to sandpaper, the factory provides the "thumb prick." This device is like a thumb tack, except that the tack is reduced to a quarter length. It is concealed by adhesive tape or a band-aid and usually attached to the underside of the thumb. Using such a device, the gambler can make miniscule indentations in salient cards, the position of which he can detect by touch. This ploy is referred to as "pegging."

Yet cheaters are never totally dependent on the factory for marking paper. Two common devices that are employed are "nailing" and "crimping," which unlike pegging, mark the cards for the sight of the reader rather than his touch. When a gambler nails the cards he uses his fingernails to mark the cards along their edges. These indentations are visible, thereby permitting the gambler to read the relevant cards for whatever game he is making. Fingernails nail, and fingers crimp. Fingernails make indentations on cards, while fingers bend them. Crimping, then, requires the dexterous bending of cards in a variety of ways so that, by sight, the gambler can discern the card that best fits his game. Nailing and crimping do not require equipment from the factory. Consequently, the use of these gimmicks depends totally upon the skill of the cheater.

All these marks are "read" by sight or by touch from

the backs of the cards. "Shiners" permit the cheater to read from the front. These are small mirrors or reflectors which may be attached to the palm of the dealer's hand, placed in pipe bowls, match boxes, in finger rings or in various places on or under the table. As cards are dealt over the shiner, values and suits are reflected, and the cheater is provided with considerable knowledge of his opponents' hands.

Strippers. Factories carry standardized stripped decks for the trade, but, like tailors, they will provide custom-made equipment for the cheater. Different cheaters may want different cards stripped, and the factory will do this for them. For example, as one factory catalogue, the source of which we shall not reveal, put it:

We are in a position to furnish special strippers made to cut any card or any combination of cards you desire. Our work is all done by men who are experts in this line of work and the tools we use are the latest and most approved type, resulting in work that is absolutely uniform and cannot be obtained elsewhere.

Most stripped decks used by cheaters are called "side strippers," "belly strippers" or "humps." These terms originate from the fact that the cards to be separated from the rest of the deck, or stripped, protrude slightly—usually one-sixteenth to one-thirty-second of an inch—from the rest of the deck. What this means is that the sucker may shuffle, and the cheater, cutting the deck, can place the stripped cards wherever he wishes in the deck. So the game is made.

The skilled cheater, however, will avoid using these gimmicks because they may be detected, and the detection may mean at least the end of his game, a beating or, in crucial games, his death. Gambling can, indeed, be a matter of life and death for the cheater as well as his mark. For example, one of our acquaintances was playing a game of poker with Filipinos. Throughout the game the Filipinos maintained a running conversation in Filipino-Spanish which the cheater did not understand. He was losing, and he immediately discerned that the Filipino players were conveying information about one another's hands in their patois. To bring an end to this, he laid a thirty-eight calibre revolver on the table and said, "The next sound I want to hear at this table is the bark from this thirty-eight." The game proceeded in silence, and the cheater made his score.

Another example would be the case of Arnold Rothstein, a well known gambler who was taken for $100,000 in a poker game. Suspecting the use of gimmicks, he refused to honor the loss and was later found shot to death. The edge of violence in card games is also demonstrated by the case of "Little Abe," otherwise known as the "Professor." Abe had his heyday in the thirties. He could make any gambling game and would often be called in to make games and take other gamblers who were disliked by insiders. One such character was a small town tough who conspicuously carried a gun at all card games. The Professor was called in to take him at twenty-one. The game had a $100 limit, and the Professor's policy was to get his opponent hooked as soon as possible so he couldn't quit the game with modest winnings. After three hours' play he had the undesirable character "in" for $10,000 (remember this was in the thirties). At that point the local tough put his gun on the table and said "I know you are doing something to me and when I find out I am going to blow your brains out." Since the Professor never used marked cards in a twenty-one game, he knew that his manipulations of the deck could never be detected. Nevertheless, he left town the next day after collecting his commission for the $12,000 he took from the tough.

Quite clearly, competence in manipulating cards is crucial in making games. Without it the cheater may be killed. On occasion even a competent cheater can be beaten or killed when his take becomes too obvious or beyond normal expectations. This depends on the temperament of the sucker coupled with the intensity of his suspicions, what some might call "paranoia." To understand the importance of this observation, imagine the consequences of incompetence displayed by a surgeon, concert pianist, or even a sociologist. Surgeons are covered by insurance. There is no insurance for the cheater. Walter Gieseking has recorded the Beethoven Emperor Concerto with an obvious error. The recording is on sale at all music stores. Were he making a card game rather than playing the piano, that might well have been the end of that illustrious pianist. Sociologists, relying as they do on computers rather than compe- tence, may publish errors in the major journals. When such errors are detected, they publicize their apologies in the same journals under a form known as Errata. Cheaters cannot apologize for mistakes. Manipulating the cards requires incredible skill and practice. Concert pianists may practice as often as six hours a day; the surgeon's practice is his surgery; and the sociologist may not practice at all. Yet, the cheater must practice up to eight hours a day before a mirror—preferably a three- way mirror—to master any given technique of manipu- lating the cards. Only when he cannot perceive his own manipulation can he establish his competence for himself and, consequently, for making future games.

Manipulating the cards takes several forms and is often a cooperative enterprise. These forms include: palming, switches, stacking, peeking and false dealing. Such manipulations of the deck sometimes require shills, for the shill can establish the impression that the cheater has not made the game but rather some apparently naive player who is in fact the cheater's ally. Thus, suspicion is diverted from the one who really makes the game. We shall not discuss the shill except insofar as he facilitates the moves of the cheater.

Palming is the substitution of the hand for the hold-out equipment we discussed earlier. Any valuable card or cards can be removed from the deck, held and reintroduced to the game at propitious stages. We have known of circumstances where as many as five cards have been palmed by cheaters, but the number is usually less, though it may on rare occasion be greater. Extreme competence is required for palming cards, since it is easily detected.

Switching and palming sometimes go together, the difference being that switching a card or cards requires the retrieval of a card from a deck in play and its exchange for some other card in the deck rather than its mere reintroduction. Palming does not require making an exchange but an exchange frequently, but not always, requires palming. Thus, one player may exchange a card in his hand for a card in his partner's hand. Or he may replace a card, cards or an entire deck of cards for a card, cards or the deck employed in the regular game.

Sometimes, then, a different deck may be exchanged for the deck in play. This is often called "cold-decking" and with good reason. Cards in play get warm, and a new deck may well be cool. The skilled gambler can detect such subtle differences in temperature. This risky manipulation may be accomplished by the cheater alone, but sometimes it requires the assistance of a shill, whose function is to distract the attention of the other players from the cheater. He too must be skilled, however. For example, he might turn on a running conversation or "chatter" at the time of the switch; or he might ask for change of a large denomination bill; or he might ask for or offer cigarettes, cigars or a light; or he might focus attention on the pot by conspicuously demanding whether everyone is "in." Such ploys disturb the continuity of the interaction and facilitate the switch.

Looking and Peeking are necessary for many manipulations of cards. Looking simply refers to the observation of cards that are revealed during the course of play or at the end of a hand. The fact that in all card games some of the cards are revealed, except in those cases, bluffing or not, where a hand is not called, is used to the advantage of the cheater or hustler, for the legitimate revelation of cards enables him to make the game. Knowing the cards that have been legitimately revealed permits the hustler to locate or anticipate the location of those same cards during the next deal.

Peeking describes the art of discerning the top or bottom card of the deck without detection by other players, although, on occasion, other cards may be discerned. Gimmicks such as shiners, to which we have referred earlier, may be used in peeking, but the skilled cheater can peek with great effectiveness without the use of any gimmick. This involves an extremely careful control of eye movement. Directly focused peeking must be perfectly timed so that what Edward Hall calls the gaze line is never interrupted. The cultivation of peripheral vision clearly enhances the art of peeking and cheaters know this very well. Above all, looking and sometimes peeking make stacking possible.

Stacking the deck is the craft of placing known cards within the deck at desired locations either prior to or during the shuffling of the deck. This insures that specific cards will be dealt to any player covertly selected by the cheater.

One need not be the dealer to stack a deck of cards. In contract bridge, for example, two decks of cards are ordinarily used in the game so that the labor of shuffling, dealing and cutting is divided. Thus, the shuffler can stack the deck for his opponent. Cutting the cards may, of course, disturb the stack and render it ineffective. This is particularly true of the "running cut," known in some circles as the "whorehouse cut." Contract bridge, however, is not usually played in whorehouses, so in that game the shuffler may slightly crimp all the cards above the line of cut. In a straight cut the unsuspecting player will quite probably cut the deck at the crimp thus returning the stack to the top of the deck. It should also be observed that, in contract bridge, the shuffler's partner makes the cut, thereby increasing the probability that the stack will be undisturbed.

Clearly, dealers do stack cards and this is often done in those games where shuffling and dealing are performed by the same player, as, for example, in poker, twenty-one and gin rummy, as well as other forms of rummy.

False Dealing. Magicians may deal cards from the center of the deck, but we know of no cheaters who do.

To our knowledge, false dealing by cheaters includes dealing "bottoms" and "seconds." Since bottom dealing is by far the most publicized—literally hundreds of American motion pictures, especially westerns, refer to it—the cheater must incur some risk in implementing this deal. Even those who play cards on occasional weekends will be looking for it; they may even have tried clumsily to experiment with it themselves. Bottom dealing is so widely known that it probably accounts for the use of the protective device of sealing the deck in such games as twenty-one and sometimes poker. What the rank amateur does not know, however, is that sealing the deck gives the skilled cheater or hustler an edge. For these gamblers can count and remember.

Second dealing is a different matter. Here the second card from the top of the deck is dealt, retaining the top card which is known to the dealer by reading or peeking. First of all, this gives the dealer an edge simply by making sure the card does not get into the game. Second, the card may be introduced into the game giving the dealer the choice of that card or some unknown card. Third, the card may be introduced into the game to destroy or bust an opponent's hand. Fourth, it may be introduced to build his shill's hand. Since fewer players will be looking for second dealing, the second dealer may enjoy a certain edge over bottom dealers in some games. However, *competent* bottom dealing is objectively as difficult to detect as *competent* second dealing.

Any hustler must know the odds in the game he is making. In draw poker, for example, the odds are four and one-half to one against making a flush by drawing one card to a four flush, or five to one against making a straight by drawing one card to an open ended straight.

Of course, it is not our purpose to recount here all the odds for improving one's hand in various games of poker. These have been systematically set down by Oswald Jacoby, one of the foremost poker, bridge and gin players in the world. The point is that *all* of these odds should be known by the full-time gambler. At the very least he must have a contextual, if not a detailed, knowledge of them.

Different techniques of estimating the odds are used in making other games of cards. Probably the currently best known of such techniques are those that have been employed by Edward O. Thorp in making the game of twenty-one, sometimes erroneously referred to as black-jack. To understand the complexity of estimating odds, we would merely observe that Thorp, a mathematician, had to employ the services of an electronic computer to "beat the dealer."

In general, knowing the odds requires not only knowing the odds for any given hand, but also relating those odds to the stakes and the size of the pot.

Stakes. Any player, before he sits in on a game, must know what the stakes are. These range from limit games (one dollar minimum, two dollar maximum, even nickel-dime poker), pot limit, where the player may bet any amount up to the amount in the pot, to table stakes, meaning that players may wager any or all of the money they have before them on the table. One's table stake can never be reduced or supplemented during a single hand. This can only be done between hands. The decision to enter a game of cards depends, to a considerable degree, on knowledge of the stakes in relation to the money that the gambler has available. With table stakes, this is crucial.

If the gambler is "down," that is, has limited funds,

he is more likely to join a lower limit game (where he can build up a larger stake) than he is to go where the action really is. Yet, in such games, his own action is limited. Of course he can cheat, but such techniques as "bluffing" and "creating a tell" are not easily employed. Bluffs can be easily called in limit games—the stakes are usually not high. Creating a tell, as we shall see, may hardly be worth the effort, since it requires a considerable investment of time and money.

With higher stakes, the options of the gambler are opened up. In the extreme, given table stakes, the gambler can merely snow the other players by bluffing at bets that they can never see or hope to call. Obviously other forms of bluffing, reverse and double-reverse psychology can be effective in games of high stakes. One such form is creating a tell. Among others, Oswald Jacoby has explained how this is done. He was challenged by an extremely wealthy and arrogant man, described as a "little tin god," to a table stake game of five-card stud poker. The challenger asserted that all bridge experts were poor poker players, since expert poker requires psychological expertise. This annoyed Jacoby. For three hours of the game Jacoby systematically piled chips on his hole card whenever it was an ace or king—losing frequently during that period. Note that it took a lot of time and money to create this tell, but at the end of the time Jacoby was certain that his opponent had taken this "obvious give-away" into account. He then changed his tactics by placing his chips only on aces, not on kings. Ultimately he took his opponent for all he had in one hand with a pair of kings over his opponent's pair of tens. The opponent was convinced that Jacoby's betting was merely a bluff, since he had not piled his chips on the king in the hole.

Pots. Quite clearly, Jacoby's move had to come at an appropriate time—when the pot was very large. Yet, he made it large. The point is that a skilled gambler must relate the stakes, the hand and the pot in making the game.

Pots as well as hands establish odds. The ratio between what is in the pot and the gambler's bet must at least equal or exceed the odds for his making the hand which he estimates will win. Otherwise he must fold. For example, if the gambler in draw poker is drawing to an open ended straight, there must be *at least* five times the amount of money in the pot that he will put up for any particular call. The same principle applies to most games of poker. In other games, for example, twenty-one, there is no pot. One merely plays against the dealer, and the relationship between hands and stakes is the critical one.

Often a skilled hustler will be identified by the gambling establishment as precisely that. The house will then take measures to prevent his play. Even the rules of the game may be changed. When Edward Thorp's system for beating twenty-one became widely publicized, the rules of that game were changed in the large gambling houses in April of 1964. The strategem was counterproductive, however. Action at the tables in Las Vegas, as well as the tourist trade, declined so sharply that the original rules were reinstituted by June of 1964. Gambling houses could not afford to lose the suckers, so they were forced to take their chances on the system players. However, recognized system players, like Thorp, were arbitrarily excluded from the action.

Consequently, identified hustlers disguise themselves. Thorp himself adopted a repertoire of disguises including hair sculpture, beards, contact lenses, sweep around sun glasses, clothing and position at the table. On the latter point, one should know that most twenty-one hustlers will sit at "third base"—the first seat on the dealer's right. To disguise his identity, Thorp would sit two seats to the right of the dealer.

These disguises are taken on to con the house, but the cheater or hustler will use disguises to con other players as well. As only one instance of this, we cite the case of a cheater who makes games of cards in the Negro ghettoes of large midwestern cities. He arrives at the scene of action in soiled bib overalls, a rumpled work shirt, scuffed work shoes, and a typical farmer's hat. He also makes sure there is a visible supply of dirt under his fingernails. He consolidates this rustic appearance with a verbal line, "I just come up from Mississippi with money I've saved so's me and my cousin can open up a chicken farm up here in the north." The players at the game will accept him willingly as a fish. He then proceeds to make the game.

As Anselm Strauss has indicated, status-forcing may at least have the consequences of pushing one up or down in some arrangement of status or in or out of participation in some social circle. Strauss' brilliant discussion, however, fails to differentiate systematically verbal from non-verbal techniques. Recently, such observers as Raymond Birdwhistell, Edward T. Hall, Robert Sommer, and Watson and Graves have considerably sharpened up the analysis of non-verbal interaction.

Now all techniques of status-forcing are extremely useful to the gambler. He may wish to build his opponent up for the big take, as in creating a tell, or he may wish to tear him down so that he loses confidence, therefore competence, in his line of play—to destroy his cool. He may wish to force a mark into a game or so control his play that he will throw in his hand or fold prematurely. The latter forcing technique, where accomplished non-verbally, has been termed "blocking" by Albert Scheflen in an outstanding general consideration of the significance of posture in communication.

One of us (Mahigel) has designed and carried out a preliminary experiment on the effects that blocking exerts on the play of poker. His findings show that the use of non-verbal techniques to control interaction in making games of cards holds great promise for establishing a significant advantage to the informed hustler.

Mahigel selected sixteen male poker-players from introductory speech classes at the University of Minnesota. These volunteers were randomly assigned to control and experimental groups, and each was asked to play three hands of draw poker with two other players who had been instructed in the experimental procedure. These latter two players blocked the play of each member of the experimental group, but not the play of members of the control group. The blocking behavior used was mild, to say the least. Each informed player, seated on either side of the experimental subject, merely placed his forearm on the card table between himself and the subject. A dealer, who did not engage in the game, dealt identical cards to all three players in each of three rounds of play, although specific hands were varied from one round to another. In other words, three hands were dealt in the first round. Each of the sixteen volunteers received the same cards, as did the two experimental assistants. In the subsequent two rounds the same procedure was followed, although different hands were dealt in each trial. When no blocking was used in 24 turns of play, there were 17 calls and 7 folds, but when blocking was used in the same number of turns, there were 11 calls and 13 folds. While these figures are not impressive in any statistical sense, they do show that an edge can be established by the gambler through manipulation of posture or body-control.

Making games of cards requires a technology—gimmicks. It also involves skill—cheating and building pots. Such skill moves into knowledge, particularly of the odds. Moreover, one must mask himself if he is very competent. Finally, seemingly insignificant gestures may make a game. In all this, we have omitted the social organization of gambling and gamblers or their universes of discourse and appearance. There are elaborate verbal and nonverbal codes used by cheaters to communicate with one another. When they find themselves together at the same tables where the action is, they can communicate all these things and more. The mark, fish, or sucker will never know. Anyone for poker?

January 1971

FURTHER READING

Mirrors and Masks by Anselm L. Strauss (Glencoe, Illinois: The Free Press, 1959).

Beat the Dealer by Edward O. Thorp (New York: Random House, 1966).

Gamble and Win by "Jack Hart" (Hollywood: Onsco Publications, 1963).

The Casino Gambler's Guide by Allan N. Wilson (New York: Harper and Row, 1970).

Part Two

SPORT

Athletes Are Not
Inferior Students

WALTER E. SCHAEFER and J. MICHAEL ARMER

Does the heavy emphasis on sports evident in most of our high schools interfere with what is supposed to be the central purpose of all high schools—education? Does sports downgrade the value that students put on intellectual effort? Does it reduce the learning of the athletes themselves?

Fewer than one out of four high-school boys play in interscholastic sports. But if we consider the immense amount of time and money spent on stadiums and gymnasiums, on teams and on their equipment and training, and on pep rallies, marching bands and cheerleading, it is easy to believe that athletics must seriously interfere with schooling. As James S. Coleman has observed, a stranger in an American high school could easily conclude that "more attention is paid to athletics by teenagers, both as athletes and as spectators, than to scholastic matters." To many observers, it has become a self-evident article of faith that athletics is overemphasized in our high schools, and that the effect of athletics is, overall, bad.

One of the difficulties with this belief, however, is that it is based on very little research. And studies that we have conducted strongly indicate that this belief is, in most respects, probably untrue. Not only does participation in sports generally seem to have little or no effect on a student's scholarship, but it seems to actually *help* certain students academically—especially those students from the poor and disadvantaged groups that usually have the most trouble in school.

The arguments of the critics run something like this:

Whatever athletics may contribute to a player's character development, sportsmanship, physical fitness, or to the pride and fame of the town, there are at least five different ways in which it interferes with the central academic objectives of a school:

☐ An excessive amount of resources, personnel and facilities of the high school is diverted from more fruitful activities.

☐ Although sports may get many parents and other adults apparently interested in school affairs, this interest is not in education itself but in a marginal activity—and therefore it may actually distract from any real educational involvement on their part.

☐ Pep rallies, trips, attending games, floats, displays and all the other paraphernalia combine to draw students away from their studies.

☐ Many potentially good students become discouraged about trying for academic excellence because the big rewards of popularity and status go to athletes and cheerleaders. Rather than being rewarded, the serious student may actually be ridiculed as a "square" and a "grind."

☐ Sports demands so much time, energy and concentration from the athletes—and gives them so much prestige compared to their studies—that their school work must inevitably suffer.

The evidence so far accumulated that might shed light on these claims is sparse. By far the most important study, in scope and in recognition, has been reported by Coleman in *The Adolescent Society*. Therefore we can use it as representative.

Let us review the evidence, point by point:

☐ *Diversion of Resources*. To our knowledge, no studies have been conducted on the extent to which the present allocation of resources, personnel and facilities to interscholastic sports in high school in fact creates a drain away from the school's academic mission. Clearly, such studies are needed. Clearly also, they would be extremely difficult to do, since no two schools or situations are alike.

☐ *Diversion of Parental Support*. Coleman's investigation of teenage culture in ten midwestern high schools focused mainly on the attitudes, values and norms of the students themselves. But a questionnaire was sent to parents, and they were asked this question: "If your son or daughter could be outstanding in high school in one of the three things listed below, which one would you want it to be?" The choices offered were "brilliant student," "athletic star" ("leader of activities" for girls) and "most popular." "Brilliant student" was chosen by more than three-fourths of the parents of boys, and over half of the parents of girls, suggesting that most parents value scholarship far more highly than athletics.

Coleman points out, however, that "these values may not be those they express day by day to their children." In fact, the responses of the students themselves to a related set of questions suggest such a discrepancy. When each student was asked how his parents would feel if he were asked to be a biology assistant, 60.2 percent of the boys responded "both would be very proud of me," and 63.5 percent of the girls gave that response. When asked how their parents would react if their children unexpectedly made the basketball team (or the cheerleading squad), 68.2 percent of the boys and 77.0 percent of the girls said both their parents would be very proud.

These data provide only very slight support, then, for the view that, in practice, parents' support of scholarship is undermined to some extent by their greater interest in athletic accomplishment.

□ *Diversion of Energy Among Student Fans.* To prove that support of school teams by the students interferes with their academic performance, one would have to demonstrate that, other things being equal, the greater the students' time and energy devoted to the support of athletics, the lower the students' academic achievement. Although such interference may well occur, there seems to be no evidence in the literature one way or the other, even in Coleman's research.

□ *Discouragement of Scholarship.* If popularity and prestige are most readily given to students for their athletic achievement, then academic achievement must be relatively unrewarded. And a high scholastic performance may well bring about the student's exclusion, scorn or ridicule. Therefore, Coleman says, the students with the most intellectual ability will know better than to try for top grades.

But again the data are not conclusive. Coleman's own figures are not clear-cut in support of his thesis—and in some cases they actually work to refute it.

In short, schools that emphasize athletics do not necessarily do so at the expense of learning; the two may actually rise or fall together. In any case, Coleman's study says nothing about the extent to which athletics, as opposed to other factors, diverts students of high ability from trying for top grades.

☐ *Diversion of Athletes Away from Scholarship.* Coleman's writings imply that an athlete's participation in sports tends to keep his scholarship down; and that athletics "recruits" many of the brightest boys and, in effect, keeps them from giving the energy and time they should to their studies. In the end, he maintains, society suffers:

> Because high schools allow adolescent societies to divert energies into athletics, social activities, and the like, they recruit into adult intellectual activities many people with a rather mediocre level of ability, and fail to attract many with high levels of ability.

Yet Coleman presents no evidence about the percentage of boys with high IQs who are in fact siphoned off this way. Moreover, studies by other researchers have showed that athletes tend, if anything, to have *better* grades than the average student.

Nevertheless, there are data and conclusions in *The Adolescent Society* that could support the view that, other things being equal, a student's participation in sports does hurt his school work. If it is true that 1) athletes do get greater social rewards (popularity, prestige, leadership) than good students; and 2) that most high-school athletes are boys; and 3) that boys value these informal rewards more than grades and promotions, or possible long-term gains (going to college, better jobs); then, true enough, boys can be expected to give as much time and energy as possible to athletics. If we further assume that time, energy and attention are limited resources, then it also follows that their studies must suffer if the boys invest these resources in athletics.

If these assumptions are stated as hypotheses, they can be put to an experimental test. For if these assumptions are true:

1. Athletes should not perform as well scholastically as nonathletes.

2. The greater the student's participation in sports, the greater the detriment to his studies.

3. A student's participation in those sports that are given the greatest recognition and attention—generally, football and basketball—should harm his academic performance more than the minor sports that do not require so much time, or give as great social rewards.

Data have now been gathered from one medium-sized and one large senior high school to test each of these hypotheses.

Mean Grade-Point Average for Athletes and
All Boys in Their Class   (Table 1)

	Mean G.P.A.*	Number
Athletes**	2.35	164
All Other Boys	1.83	421

* Grade-point averages are based on the following scale: A=4, B=3, C=2, D=1, F=0. Each student's G.P.A. is based on his final marks in all major courses during the six semesters of his three-year high school. (Physical education is not included as a major course.) G.P.A.s may be based on anywhere from one to six semesters, depending on how long the student remained in school.
** Boys who completed at least one full season as a member of an inter-scholastic athletic team are classified as athletes.

In Table 1 we have compared the grade-point averages (A=4=excellent, B=3=good, C=2=fair, D=1=passing, F=0=failure) of 585 boys in the two high schools, contrasting the athletes and nonathletes. Clearly, *the athletes obtained better grades*. The athletes, on the average, got over C, the nonathletes got less than C. There may, of course, be many reasons for this finding, apart from the students' participation in sports. Athletes could start high school with a greater potential or motivation, and get higher grades not because of but *despite* athletics, and so on. But even when we control for these intitial differences, by matching athletes with nonathletes, we still find the athletes getting slightly higher grades. (See Table 2.)

Mean G.P.A. of Athletes and Matched
Nonathletes & Percentage of Athletes Who
Exceed Their Matches in G.P.A.   (Table 2)

	Mean G.P.A.	Percent of Athletes Higher Than Match	Number
Athletes	2.35		152
		56.6	
Matched Nonathletes	2.24		152

☐ *Variation by Amount of Participation.* What about the effects of *amount* of participation in sports? Dividing the athletes into those who completed one or two seasons on the one hand, and those who completed three or more on the other, again we found that the results did not support the hypothesis. The more the athletes participated in sports, the greater the positive gap between their grades and those of their matched nonathletes. (See Table 3.) The difference between the grades of the less-active athletes and their matches was

Percentages of Athletes with Higher, Same, & Lower G.P.A.s Than Their Matches, & Mean G.P.A.s of Both Groups by Amount of Participation

(Table 3)

Amt. of Participation	With Higher G.P.A.		Percentage of Athletes With Same G.P.A.	With Lower G.P.A.		Total	Number of Pairs	Mean G.P.A.	
	.25 or more diff.	.01 to .24 diff.		-.01 to -.24 diff.	-.25 or more diff.			Athletes	Matched Non-athletes
Three or More Seasons	48.8%	11.6%	1.2%	10.5%	27.9%	100%	86	2.45	2.24
(Total)	*(60.4%)*		*(1.2%)*		*(38.4%)*	*(100%)*			
One or Two Seasons	37.9%	13.6%	3.0%	9.1%	36.4%	100%	66	2.26	2.23
(Total)	*(51.5%)*		*(3.0%)*		*(35.5%)*	*(100%)*			

.03. Between more-active athletes and their matches, the difference was .18—six times as much.

Viewed another way, 51.5 percent of the less active athletes exceeded their matches, compared with 60.4 percent of the more active athletes. Again, rather than eroding academic performance, extensive participation in interscholastic sports seems to slightly increase a student's scholastic success.

☐ *Variation by Type of Sport.* According to the prediction, playing football or basketball would hurt a student's grades more than playing in minor sports, such as track, swimming, wrestling and gymnastics, in which the rewards, effort and competition might be less. Table 4 clearly shows that, while participants in the two major sports have somewhat lower average G.P.A.s than participants in minor sports, those in major sports exceed their matches to a greater extent than those in

---

Mean G.P.A. for Athletes & Matched Nonathletes, & Percentage of Athletes Who Exceed Their Match in G.P.A., by Type of Sport   (Table 4)

Type of Sport	Mean G.P.A.	Percent of Athletes Higher Than Match	Number
Major Sport*			
Athlete	2.20		83
		60.2	
Matched Nonathlete	2.02		83
Minor Sport**			
Athlete	2.53		69
		52.1	
Matched Nonathlete	2.50		69

* Major sports include football and basketball, according to our coding criteria. Participants in major sports sometimes participated in one or more minor sports also, but the reverse is never true, according to these criteria.
** Minor sports in both schools include baseball, track, cross-country, swimming, wrestling, tennis, and golf; the larger school also fields teams in gymnastics and in hockey.

minor sports do. Therefore, the prediction does not hold up.

□ *Variations Among Types of Boys.* Having found no support so far for the various "interference" hypotheses, we can now legitimately ask whether the major prediction holds true among any of the boys. For instance, does participation in athletics have a greater positive effect on academic achievement among white-collar boys than among blue-collar boys? Among high IQ boys than low IQ boys? Among college-bound boys than work-bound boys? Or among high achievers than low achievers in junior high school?

The data in Table 5 reveal two clear patterns. First, the slight positive association between athletics and scholarship persists in all subgroups. In no case is the relationship negative. More than half the athletes in each category exceed their matches, and the average GPA of athletes is always higher than that of their matched nonathletes. Moreover, on father's occupation and curriculum, the gap is greater between athletes and their matches in the lower categories than in the higher. For example, greater percentages of blue-collar athletes than white-collar athletes exceed their matches in GPA (63.0 percent versus 53.7 percent). An even greater spread separates non-college-preparatory athletes from college-preparatory athletes (69.0 percent versus 53.7 percent).

In short, the boys who would usually have the most trouble in school are precisely the ones who seem to benefit most from taking part in sports.

□ *Interpretation.* These findings, of course, do not tell us whether athletics diverts a high school's resources, staff manhours and facilities at the expense of the scholastic program; whether the support of parents is channeled away from education; whether the academic

Mean G.P.A. for Athletes & Matched Nonathletes & Percentage of Athletes Who Exceed Their Match in G.P.A., by Father's Occupation, Intelligence-Test Score, Curriculum, & G.P.A. for Last Semester of Junior High School

(Table 5)

Characteristic	Mean G.P.A.	Percent of Athletes Higher Than Match	Number
Father's Occupation			
White Collar			
Athlete	2.53		95
		53.7	
Matched Nonathlete	2.48		95
Blue Collar			
Athlete	2.05		54
		63.0	
Matched Nonathlete	1.84		54
Intelligence-Test Scores			
Upper Half of Class			
Athlete	2.64		94
		56.4	
Matched Nonathlete	2.55		94
Lower Half of Class			
Athlete	1.88		58
		56.9	
Matched Nonathlete	1.74		58
Curriculum			
College Preparatory			
Athlete	2.47		123
		53.7	
Matched Nonathlete	2.40		123
Non-college Preparatory			
Athlete	1.85		29
		69.0	
Matched Nonathlete	1.56		29
G.P.A. for Last Semester of Junior High School			
Upper Half of Class			
Athlete	2.82		78
		57.7	
Matched Nonathlete	2.70		78
Lower Half of Class			
Athlete	1.85		74
		55.4	
Matched Nonathlete	1.75		74

achievement of student fans suffers from their support of school teams; or whether potentially top students are discouraged from trying because social rewards go to athletes instead.

But these findings do bring into serious question the notion prevalent among many teachers, parents and social scientists that the supposed overemphasis on athletics in the American high schools results in the lowering of academic achievement among athletes. At the very least, the data cast doubt on the validity of Jules Henry's irate judgment that "athletics, popularity, and mediocre grades go together with inarticulateness and poor grammar."

If there is in fact a positive effect of participation in athletics on grades, as the data suggest, why does it occur? Here we are forced to speculate.

1. Perhaps athletes are graded more leniently, because teachers see them as special or more deserving.

2. Perhaps exposure, in the sports subculture, to effort, hard work, persistence and winning spills over into nonathletic activities, such as schoolwork.

3. Perhaps the superior physical condition of athletes improves their mental performance.

4. Perhaps some athletes strive to get good grades to be eligible for certain sports.

5. Perhaps athletes make more efficient and effective use of their limited study time.

6. Perhaps the lure of a college career in sports motivates some athletes to strive for good grades.

7. Perhaps the higher prestige that students obtain from sports gives them a better self-concept and higher aspirations in other activities, such as schoolwork.

8. Perhaps athletes benefit from more help in schoolwork from friends, teachers and parents.

Why does participation in athletics appear to have its greatest positive effect on the academic performance of those boys with blue-collar backgrounds and a non-college-preparatory label? A plausible interpretation of this finding is that, compared to nonathletes with the same characteristcs, blue-collar and non-college-bound athletes are more likely to associate and identify with white-collar and college-bound members of the school's leading crowd. Illustrative cases are abundant of blue-collar boys who were not at all academically-oriented or college-oriented until they began to "make it" in sports, and to be increasingly influenced by white-collar boys (and girls) with whom they would not otherwise have associated or identified.

Another important type of educational achievement is graduation from high school. Does participation in interscholastic sports keep boys in school? The data presented in Table 6 strongly suggest a Yes answer. Whereas 9.2 percent of the matched nonathletes dropped out of school before graduating, less than one-fourth as many (2.0 percent) of the athletes failed to finish. (These figures do not include boys who transferred to another school.)

Percentage of Athletes & Matched Nonathletes
Who Dropped Out of School
Before Graduation   (Table 6)

	Percent	Number
Athletes	2.0	152
Matched Nonathletes	9.2	152

This finding suggests that athletics exerts a holding influence on students, which might operate in four different ways. First, the high prestige that athletes are likely to receive probably makes them want to remain in school. Second, athletes who are potential dropouts are likely to associate and identify with college-oriented (or at least graduation-oriented) boys more often than are nonathletes who are potential dropouts. Third, some athletes might stay in school simply to be able to participate in high-school sports—or, later, college or professional sports. Fourth, potential dropouts who are athletes are likely to get encouragement and counseling from coaches and others, while nonathletic potential dropouts are likely to get much less encouragement from anybody.

Whatever the reasons, it is clear that participation in athletics exerts a holding influence over some boys who otherwise might have dropped out. Of the nine matched nonathletes who dropped out with GPAs of below 2.0, eight could be paired with athletes who ended up with equal or lower GPAs but did not drop out. This finding provides limited support for Coleman's suggestion that "if it were not for interscholastic athletics. . . the rate of dropout might be far worse. . . ."

An assertion often heard, but little studied, is that competitive sports serve as an important vehicle for upward mobility. Numerous examples can be cited, of course, of college or professional athletes' having risen above their fathers in income and status solely or primarily because of athletic achievements.

We know of no prior systematic studies in the United States, however, to determine how often this is true. Yet information about the relationship between a student's participation in interscholastic athletics and his expectations of attending college is of interest for two reasons: It provides a basis for understanding the role of athletics in upward mobility, insofar as mobility is dependent on someone's attending and graduating from college; and it provides additional data about the extent to which athletics impedes or facilitates the attainment of one of high school's educational goals—to send a maximum number of youths to college.

Pertinent data on this point have been gathered from questionnaires filled out by 785 twelfth-grade boys in three public and three Catholic high schools in three middle-sized (50,000 to 100,000) Pennsylvania cities during the spring of 1965. (See "Participation in Interscholastic Athletics and College Expectations," Richard A. Rehberg and Walter E. Schafer, *The American Journal of Sociology*, LXXIII, 1968.) Among other things, the boys were asked to name the extra-curricular activities they participated in during their senior years, how far they expected to go in college, their fathers' education and occupation and how often their parents encouraged them to go to college. The students' rank in their graduating classes was obtained from school records.

College Expectation of Athletes & All
Other Boys in Their Class   (Table 7)

| | Percent who expect to complete . . . | | |
	at least two years of college	at least four years of college	Number
Athletes	82	62	284
All Other Boys	75	45	490

Table 7 shows that, in comparison with nonathletes, athletes are slightly more likely to expect to complete at least two years of college (82 percent versus 75 percent), and considerably more likely to expect to complete at least four years of college (62 percent versus 45 percent). And if we hold the factors of background and early ability and aspirations about equal, we still get the same results. (See Table 8.)

College Expectations of Athletes & All Other
Boys in Their Class—With Controls   (Table 8)

| | Percent who expect to complete . . . | | |
	at least two years of college	at least four years of college	Number
Athletes	80	61	284
All Other Boys	76	45	490

Note: Social status, the amount of encouragement from parents, and the students' rank in their graduating classes have been controlled for.

To what extent participation in athletics directly causes higher educational expectations is, of course, still open to question; but there is little doubt that more athletes intend to go to college than matched non-athletes. Earlier, we noted that higher scholastic achievement was especially marked among athletes who were from working-class backgrounds and who were not college bound. Are expectations of attending college, therefore, relatively more common among athletes who are less "earmarked" for college? Our findings indicate that the answer is Yes. (See Table 9.) That is, a greater percentage of athletes than nonathletes expect to complete four years of college among working-class rather than middle-class boys; among boys with less, rather than more, parental encouragement; and among boys in the lower rather than the upper half of their graduating classes.

It would seem, then, that interscholastic athletics serves a democratizing or equalizing function. It represents a vehicle for upward mobility, especially of those

College Expectations of Athletes & All Other Boys in
Their Class, by Social Status, Parental Education
Encouragement & Rank in Graduating Class   (Table 9)

| | Percent who expect to complete . . . | | |
Characteristic	at least two years of college	at least four years of college	Number
Social Status			
Middle			
Athletes	91	78	90
All Other Boys	89	67	144
Working			
Athletes	78	55	194
All Other Boys	69	36	346
Parental Educational Encouragement			
High			
Athletes	90	68	208
All Other Boys	88	56	298
Low			
Athletes	58	45	66
All Other Boys	55	26	164
Rank in Graduating Class			
High			
Athletes	94	85	116
All Other Boys	89	78	205
Low			
Athletes	74	46	164
All Other Boys	66	21	280

otherwise not likely to complete college. And the data
suggest that, at least as far as participants are concerned,
athletics fosters rather than interferes with the educational goal of sending a maximum number of youth to
college.

The question arises whether all of these findings
apply to Negro boys. We know that sports is an
important channel to success for many Negroes, but we
do not know *how* important, or to what extent it varies

in time and place. Nor do we know how often Negro boys put all their hopes into becoming a Willie Mays, Wilt Chamberlain or Bob Hayes in college or professional sports, but fail, and end up disillusioned and unprepared for more conventional routes of mobility.

In this article, we could not deal with the results of a student's relative success in sports. Obviously, athletics will affect the star and the substitute differently. Success means greater prestige; and this might mean higher self-regard, higher aspirations and higher academic performance. On the other hand, it might mean more praise and distraction than most teenage boys can handle and still do good school work.

It is a frequent claim of coaches, playground directors and Little League promoters that athletics deters students from deviance within the school and delinquency in the community. Over 30 years ago, Willard Waller noted that many teachers deliberately supported interscholastic sports because they felt that it

> makes students more teachable because it drains off their surplus energies and leaves them less inclined to get into mischief. . . . Part of the technique, indeed, of those who handle difficult cases consists in getting those persons interested in . . . athletics.

But we don't really know. Again, it seems that nobody has systematically investigated the problem.

A striking feature of varsity sports—college and high school—is the great authority of the coach in controlling the athletes' off-the-field behavior. The coach usually has the unquestioned authority to suspend or drop a boy from the team if he is caught smoking, drinking, staying out too late or violating a law. Some coaches even decide the hair styles, dress, friendship patterns and the language of their boys. A few "training rules," of course, are laid down for the sake of the athletes' physical conditioning and efficiency, but others can be understood only as part of the "moralism" associated with sports. The high-school athlete is supposed to be a "good American boy." A fascinating question for research, therefore, is: What are the long-term effects on the athlete from this rigid and often puritanical control by coaches? A related question: Does high-school sports really contribute to the "character development" that coaches so often claim?

Finally, what of the lifetime and career effects of a student's participation in athletics, after he has left high school and even college? Of course, many examples can be cited of individuals who have been successful through sports—either by staying in as players or coaches, or through the education or contacts that sports has made possible. But what of the others? And what are the direct and indirect factors and mechanisms involved?

These are all matters that call for careful and rigorous research. Clearly, interscholastic athletics is far more important in the American educational process—for good or ill—than most social scientists seem to want to recognize. And the extent of that importance cannot be determined by the unsupported rhetoric of those who have personal reasons to applaud, or denounce, high-school athletics.

November 1968

FURTHER READING

The Adolescent Society by James S. Coleman (New York: The Free Press of Glencoe, Inc., 1961). A large-scale study that describes the central place of athletics in the subculture of American adolescents.

Sport and Society by Peter McIntosh (New York: International

Publishing Service, 1963). A comprehensive and suggestive work on a variety of sociological aspects of athletics.

Sport: Mirror of American Life by Robert H. Boyle (Boston: Little, Brown and Co., 1963). A journalistic account, abundant with sociological insights, of sport in America. Includes an excellent discussion of the Negro in sport.

"Participation in Interscholastic Athletics and Delinquency: A Preliminary Study," by Walter E. Schafer in *Social Problems* (Summer, 1969), pp. 40-47.

"Athletic Participation, College Aspirations and College Encouragement" by Walter E. Schafer and Richard A. Rehberg in *Pacific Sociological Review*, Vol. 13, No. 3 (Summer, 1970), pp. 182-186.

Athletics for Athletes by Jack Scott, (Berkeley: Other Ways Books, 1969.)

"A Longitudinal Analysis of the Relationship Between High School Student Values, Social Participation, and Educational-Occupational Achievement" by Eldon Snyder in *Sociology of Education*, Vol. 42, No. 3 (Summer, 1969), pp. 261-270.

"Lament the Letterman: Effects of Peer Status and Extra-curricular Activities on Goals and Achievement" by William G. Spady in *American Journal of Sociology*, Vol. 75, No. 4, Part 2 (January, 1970), pp. 680-702.

The Affluent Baseball Player

RALPH ANDREANO

The major-league ball player himself sometimes contributes to the desecration of his image as a special sort of folk hero. His public preoccupation with future security in the form of a valuable early-retirement pension makes him a mere transient idol. He prefers business contracts to the camaraderie of fans. Instead of endorsing Mother, the Flag, and Little Leaguers, he promotes merchandise on national television that makes him no more than equal to the average shaver, B.O. sufferer, or fungus-footed shoe clerk.

Jim Brosnan, "The Fantasy World of Baseball,"
Atlantic Monthly, April 1964.

Modern baseball players have changed; they are, like all other Americans, interested in home, security and the good things of life. One gets the impression that this is a new social value, that ball players of an early era were more interested in the "game" and not in the money. In part this shift is true, but it would be misleading to wholeheartedly classify modern ball players as "money-hungry." Today's ball players just have a much broader base of income-producing possibilities than those of other eras. Today's players tend to be much more educated and have better post-playing opportunities; most of them do not view major league baseball primarily as a rung in the ladder of social and economic mobility. This latter factor is still inherent in baseball, of course (primarily in the case of ball players from underprivileged minority groups), but it is not the dominant outlet it once was for American youth.

One of the most startling differences between today's major league ball player and those of earlier periods is in education. Of the 497 players listed in the *Sporting News Baseball Register* for 1963, some 200, or roughly 40 percent had attended a junior college, college or university for at least one semester or more, and a fair number had graduated. About 50 percent of the managers had attended or graduated from some institution of higher learning. With respect to coaches the college-educated group was about 25 percent. The future stock of players seems today to be more intimately related to colleges and universities than historically has been the case. These figures also suggest that the quality and type of young man who enters the labor pool of baseball players has changed significantly over time. This is not to imply that ball players today tend to be intellectuals disguised in gray flannels, although there are a number of quite interesting cases of literate and articulate men who are major league ball players, but, rather, that the supplying institutions for the major leagues have shifted to reflect the much higher prestige attached to education.

The carriers of heroic legend of earlier baseball were

men from the semiliterate, poverty-stricken pockets of
the nation who fought their way to the big time. A
seemingly inexhaustible supply of folk heroes existed
with whom generations of fans could unreservedly
identify. But today it is rare when a star major league
ball player rises from some rural or urban slum. Negroes
and Latin American players are, of course, exceptions.
But in both cases the close identification between
spectator and player that characterized earlier baseball is
almost entirely absent because the roots of social
rejection go too deep. There are no more Babe Ruths,
Ty Cobbs, Joe DiMaggios.

The relevance of this apparent change in the social
origins of today's baseball players is that the appeals
made by organized baseball to young men must be
refocused; they must not only emphasize the inherent
qualities that attract men into the game, but also appeal
to the game's sense of professional accomplishment. The
change in educational attainment reflects both the
relatively short earning span of ball players, on the one
hand, and the much greater demands that the modern
American economy places on potential workers in their
middle or late thirties, requiring them to have some
educational background, training and skills. The modern
ball player tends to be one who does indeed have
something to rely on when his playing days are over.

Organized baseball has recognized this change in
educational requirements in an elegantly prepared publicity brochure called, "Baseball, The Game, The Career,
The Opportunity." Here, it is pointed out to potential
major league baseball players that the requirements of
education and a long-term life career need not interfere
with participation in organized baseball. Listed in this
brochure, along with schools offering scholarship plans

for baseball players, are more than 1,100 colleges and universities which will accept students on a part-time basis. The implication is that a young man can play major league baseball and still acquire the educational prerequisities necessary to his post-baseball career. As explained in the brochure:

> Further along in this book you will come across players who have benefited tremendously from combining the years in baseball with the pursuit of an education. There are a great many such men who, of course, could not be included in this book. . . . Nowhere else can there be found the number of access roads to success that baseball offers the qualified young man.

Though no systematic sampling of post-baseball careers has been undertaken, it is offered as a generalization here that the greater fraction of ball players in past generations has tended to find post-playing occupations within the structure of professional baseball. The average playing life of a major league player is about seven years, and though the degree of specialization today may tend to lengthen this average, the post-playing opportunities would not appear to be drastically changed as a result. With greater education, however, today's ball player may, over the next generation, assume fewer post-playing opportunities within the professional game. Some glimpse of employment opportunities was obtained by an analysis of the playing rosters of the 1941 pennant winners, the New York Yankees and the Brooklyn Dodgers. As of October 1963, out of a total of 47 eligible ball players, 16 were still earning all their income from baseball, 13 were self-employed or worked in business outside baseball, 9 had service-type jobs outside of baseball, nothing was known about 7 players, and 2 were radio and TV announcers of major league games.

A recent survey of the teams of both major leagues showed that the feeding ground for major ball players conforms quite closely to the nation's population configuration, with one exception: the disproportionately large share contributed by the states of the South and Southwest. California, New York, Pennsylvania and Illinois, which are the four most populous states, and Michigan, which ranks seventh, together contribute 267 (one-third) of the nation's major league ball players. (California, second in population, contributes 90.)

But the states of the South and Southwest, with lesser populations, contribute 32 percent, and foreign-born players make up 8.4 percent—together 60 more players than the five most productive states. What does this mean? Is baseball still a major route of social and economic mobility for underprivileged groups, racial as well as economic? Does an affluent society—viz. Pennsylvania, New York, California—produce a differently motivated ball player than Mississippi? From the *Sporting News Baseball Register* for 1963, I calculated that there were 49 American Negroes in the major leagues and 35 came from the states of the South and Southwest. As a group, American-born Negroes were roughly 10 percent of the total major league roster in 1963; few American-born Negroes are pitchers and none are managers. (It always has seemed strange to me that major league baseball received immense credit for accepting Negroes as players but only two persons have cracked the managerial caste-system as coaches.)

In practice, a salary is the only major issue to be negotiated at year's end between player and management; under the reserve rule, a player wishing to play must do so for the team owning his contract. By agreement, a player cannot be cut more than 25 percent over the previous year's salary; there is no agreement with regard to the size of an increase. Evaluating the individual player is the most difficult of all tasks facing the management. In purely economic terms one would expect a player to receive a salary commensurate to his relative importance to the team; either for his specific skill as it contributes to the overall success of the team, or in some cases, for his popularity and gate-appeal in relation to the total attendance and revenue accruing to the team over a pennant season.

But measuring individual value can become most arbitrary. The salaries of individual players historically have reflected both the difficulty in specifically judging a player's worth and the wide variation in bargaining strength of individual players. The first professional major league team to employ salaried players, the Cincinnati Red Stockings of 1869, did not pay higher than $1,500 per man. During the 1880s, major league ball players' salaries ranged between $1,000 and $5,000 with the median salary probably around $3,000 for a seven-month season. Relative to unskilled workers in the manufacturing sector of the economy, major league ball players of the last quarter of the nineteenth century were well paid for their special skills. Of course, whether or not such players were being paid at rates equivalent to their market value is not possible to determine, though some inferential evidence suggests that this was not the case. The legendary pitcher, Cy Young, for example, had a yearly salary in the 1890-1900 period which never exceeded $2,400. The so-called greatest baseball team of all time, the 1927 New York Yankees (Ruth, Gehrig) paid a median salary of $7,000 and an arithmetic average salary of $10,000. Babe Ruth's salary tends to inflate the average figures, so that the median salary is probably a much more reasonable approximation to compensation levels of this great team.

Players then, as today, tended to have supplementary sources of income during the off-season so that their average yearly incomes were much higher. Considering only income earned from playing ball, however, the wage trends of major league ball players show a marked upward rise between 1910 and 1930.

During the depression of the 1930s the absolute level of major league salaries fell drastically, although the extent of the fall varied considerably from team to team. Relative to changes in the cost of living and wage declines in other parts of the economy, however, the wage picture for major league ball players was not so bad. A comparison of baseball receipts, industry sales in manufacturing, and a cost of living index reveals that real wages in baseball during the bottom point of the depression were higher than in 1929. Real wages continued to rise during the depression.

Ball players' salaries tended to lag in real terms during World War II; the prewar upward trend leveled off in the postwar decades so that between 1950 and 1963 the real value of total wage payments declined about 10 percent. Minor league salaries are, of course, well below those of major league ball players.

As indicated earlier, other sources of income are readily available to most active major league ball players. TV endorsements, radio and television interviews and appearances, picture endorsements on bubble-gum cards, and the after-dinner speakers tour are all sources of additional income. Many players have also appeared as entertainers and actors during the off season and most have some form of steady employment (or business) in which either the advertising value of their baseball name or their personal contacts make them valuable employees and businessmen.

One of the most lucrative sources of wage supplements available to ball players on pennant winning teams and teams in the first division is their player share of World Series receipts. These shares have been gradually increasing and in the 1963 season the players' share (based on receipts for the first four games) reached an all-time high, $1,017,546.

Supplementary benefits are also comfortable for major league ball players today, though this was certainly not always the case. The players' pension fund and hospitalization and sick benefits are very respectable compared to similar funds in private industry. Receipts for the fund come from All-Star Games, part of World Series revenue, and individual payments from players. Monthly retirement benefits under the plan vary with the number of years of credited service in the major leagues (the minimum for qualifying is five years).

Against this general background of compensation levels, it may be fruitful to explore the question of whether or not professional baseball players are "exploited" because of the reserve clause (by which a player's services are held in perpetual option by the team owning his contract). Exploitation in strict economic terms would exist when a worker receives less in wage and supplementary payments than his contribution to total output. This would be difficult to determine either way for professional ball players. The median salary of major leaguers in 1950 ($11,000) and at present ($13,000 at a guess) compare very favorably with wage payments in recreation industries (excluding

motion pictures) and with median incomes of physi-
cians, lawyers and dentists.

Professional ball players are the first to deny that the
peculiar bargaining situation of their labor market
results in their being exploited. Certainly, public statements by ball players leave one with the impression that
they are not impressed with arguments concerning their
peonage. Most recently Bob Friend, a player representative to the National League, commented on an article
which suggested that unionization was the only hope for
professional ball players if they wished to elevate their
status: "During the 13 years I have been in the major
league, I know of no player who has been exploited."

Friend's attitude, as that of all ball players, is
perfectly rational when they are considered as folk
heroes. Perpetuation of the mythical qualities of professional major league ball players requires that they, as
well as the institutions of the game, be kept separate
and distinct from the mainstream of American industrial
organization. It is a gross failure, I believe, on the part
of critics of organized baseball to overlook the peculiar
attachment ball players have to their historical role as
folk heroes—as people somehow ingrained in the American tradition, but yet apart from it. Bob Friend's
reaction is typical:

> If the structure of our players' association was
> changed to a union, I believe it would result in ill will
> for the players. It would tend to destroy the image of
> the baseball star for the youngsters because of the
> haggling between the players and the owners. Stan
> Musial picketing a ball park would look great,
> wouldn't it?

The hero worship syndrome which the adulation of
the major league ball player represents in American life

is the key to understanding the special and unique administrative and market structure of professional baseball. A ball player feels direct and psychic association with the legendary players of the past; he is a part of American history and therefore above the din of the average guy who works for a weekly or hourly wage.

What is at issue here, then is not that the status of ball players can be improved by their engaging in the process of collective bargaining, though under certain conditions this would indeed be beneficial. The issue, rather, is the dilemma of the modern ball player. On the one hand, he is expected to be satisfied with his moderate financial position, which is in keeping with his position of folk hero. On the other hand, he is attracted by the typically American enticements of extra money for endorsements, retirement security, etc. As a modern man he is better educated and is more seriously concerned about planning a constructive life for himself after his retirement from baseball; yet as a folk hero he is expected to be innocent, fun-loving and willing to sacrifice material security and future plans for The Game. The ball player has gained status through the perpetuation of these myths. Now he has reached an impasse; for to try to reap the material benefits of his status means necessarily to destroy the myths.

The ad agencies show little enough imagination in the way they hire the ball players to act as hucksters. Americans do not resent affluence but they do resent crass insincerity. But baseball management is equally culpable for insisting that the ball player project an image completely inoffensive to all segments of the population. The ball player's image is made primarily on the playing field, and it is here that the player's acceptance of the organization-man role hurts his (and the game's) future. If players fail to see that their role as folk heroes is endangered by the homogenization of their personalities by club owners then one can only hope that the club owners will. It seems incredible that Jim Brosnan was prohibited from publishing his writing during the playing season but that Mickey Mantle could do shaving cream ads on TV.

May/June 1965

This article comes from the author's book *No Joy in Mudville*, Schenkman Publishing Company, Cambridge, Mass., © 1965.

Magic in Professional Baseball

GEORGE GMELCH

We find magic wherever the elements of chance and accident, and the emotional play between hope and fear have a wide and extensive range. We do not find magic wherever the pursuit is certain, reliable, and well under the control of rational methods.

Bronislaw Malinowski

Professional baseball is a nearly perfect arena in which to test Malinowski's hypothesis about magic. The great anthropologist was not, of course, talking about sleight of hand but of rituals, taboos and fetishes that men resort to when they want to ensure that things go their own way. Baseball is rife with this sort of magic, but, as we shall see, the players use it in some aspects of the game far more than in others.

Everyone knows that there are three essentials of baseball—hitting, pitching and fielding. The point is, however, that the first two, hitting and pitching, involve

128

a high degree of chance. The pitcher is the player least able to control the outcome of his own efforts. His best pitch may be hit for a bloop single while his worst pitch may be hit directly to one of his fielders for an out. He may limit the opposition to a single hit and lose, or he may give up a dozen hits and win. It is not uncommon for pitchers to perform well and lose, and vice versa; one has only to look at the frequency with which pitchers end a season with poor won-lost percentages but low earned run averages (number of runs given up per game). The opposite is equally true: some pitchers play poorly, giving up many runs, yet win many games. In brief, the pitcher, regardless of how well he performs, is dependent upon the proficiency of his teammates, the inefficiency of the opposition and the supernatural (luck).

But luck, as we all know, comes in two forms, and many fans assume that the pitcher's tough losses (close games in which he gave up very few runs) are eventually balanced out by his "lucky" wins. This is untrue, as a comparison of pitchers' lifetime earned run averages to their overall won-lost records shows. If the player could apply a law of averages to individual performance, there would be much less concern about chance and uncertainty in baseball. Unfortunately, he cannot and does not.

Hitting, too, is a chancy affair. Obviously, skill is required in hitting the ball hard and on a line. Once the ball is hit, however, chance plays a large role in determining where it will go, into a waiting glove or whistling past a falling stab.

With respect to fielding, the player has almost complete control over the outcome. The average fielding percentage or success rate of .975, compared to a .245

success rate for hitters (the average batting average), reflects the degree of certainty in fielding. Next to the pitcher or hitter, the fielder has little to worry about when he knows that better than 9.7 times in ten he will execute his task flawlessly.

If Malinowski's hypothesis is correct, we should find magic associated with hitting and pitching, but none with fielding. Let us take the evidence by category—ritual, taboo and fetish.

Ritual: After each pitch, ex-major leaguer Lou Skeins used to reach into his back pocket to touch a crucifix, straighten his cap and clutch his genitals. Detroit Tiger infielder Tim Maring wore the same clothes and put them on exactly in the same order each day during a batting streak. Baseball rituals are almost infinitely various. After all, the ballplayer can ritualize any activity he considers necessary for a successful perform-ance, from the type of cereal he eats in the morning to the streets he drives home on.

Usually, rituals grow out of exceptionally good performances. When the player does well he cannot really attribute his success to skill alone. He plays with the same amount of skill one night when he gets four hits as the next night when he goes hitless. Through magic, such as ritual, the player seeks greater control over his performance, actually control over the elements of chance. The player, knowing that his ability is fairly constant, attributes the inconsistencies in his per-formance to some form of behavior or a particular food that he ate. When a player gets four hits in a game, especially "cheap" hits, he often believes that there must have been something he did, in addition to his ability, that shifted luck to his side. If he can attribute his good fortune to the glass of iced tea he drank before the game or the new shirt he wore to the ballpark, then by repeating the same behavior the following day he can hope to achieve similar results. (One expression of this belief is the myth that eating certain foods will give the ball "eyes," that is, a ball that seeks the gaps between fielders.) In hopes of maintaining a batting streak, I once ate fried chicken every day at 4:00 P.M., kept my eyes closed during the national anthem and changed sweat shirts at the end of the fourth inning each night for seven consecutive nights until the streak ended.

Fred Caviglia, Kansas City minor league pitcher, explained why he eats certain foods before each game: "Everything you do is important to winning. I never forget what I eat the day of a game or what I wear. If I pitch well and win I'll do it all exactly the same the next day I pitch. You'd be crazy not to. You just can't ever tell what's going to make the difference between winning and losing."

Rituals associated with hitting vary considerably in complexity from one player to the next, but they have several components in common. One of the most popular is tagging a particular base when leaving and returning to the dugout each inning. Tagging second base on the way to the outfield is habitual with some players. One informant reported that during a successful month of the season he stepped on third base on his way to the dugout after the third, sixth and ninth innings of each game. Asked if he ever purposely failed to step on the bag he replied, "Never! I wouldn't dare, it would destroy my confidence to hit." It is not uncommon for a hitter who is playing poorly to try different combinations of tagging and not tagging particular bases in an attempt to find a successful combination. Other components of a hitter's ritual may include tapping the plate with his bat a precise number of times or taking a precise number of warm-up swings with the leaded bat.

One informant described a variation of this in which he gambled for a certain hit by tapping the plate a fixed number of times. He touched the plate once with his bat for each base desired: one tap for a single, two for a double and so on. He even built in odds that prevented him from asking for a home run each time. The odds of hitting a single with one tap were one in three, while the chances of hitting a home run with four taps were one in 12.

Clothing is often considered crucial to both hitters and pitchers. They may have several athletic supporters and a number of sweat shirts with ritual significance. Nearly all players wear the same uniform and undergarments each day when playing well, and some even wear the same street clothes. In 1954, the New York Giants, during a 16-game winning streak, wore the same clothes in each game and refused to let them be cleaned for fear that their good fortune might be washed away with the dirt. The route taken to and from the stadium can also have significance; some players drive the same streets to the ballpark during a hitting streak and try different routes during slumps.

Because pitchers only play once every four days, the rituals they practice are often more complex than the hitters', and most of it, such as tugging the cap between pitches, touching the rosin bag after each bad pitch or smoothing the dirt on the mound before each new batter, takes place on the field. Many baseball fans have observed this behavior never realizing that it may be as important to the pitcher as throwing the ball.

Dennis Grossini, former Detroit farmhand, practiced the following ritual on each pitching day for the first three months of a winning season. First, he arose from bed at exactly 10:00 A.M. and not a minute earlier or later. At 1:00 P.M. he went to the nearest restaurant for two glasses of iced tea and a tuna fish sandwich. Although the afternoon was free, he observed a number of taboos such as no movies, no reading and no candy. In the clubhouse he changed into the sweat shirt and jock he wore during his last winning game, and one hour before the game he chewed a wad of Beechnut chewing tobacco. During the game he touched his letters (the team name on his uniform) after each pitch and straightened his cap after each ball. Before the start of each inning he replaced the pitcher's rosin bag next to the spot where it was the inning before. And after every inning in which he gave up a run he went to the clubhouse to wash his hands. I asked him which part of the ritual was most important. He responded: "You can't really tell what's most important so it all becomes important. I'd be afraid to change anything. As long as I'm winning I do everything the same. Even when I can't wash my hands [this would occur when he must bat] it scares me going back to the mound . . . . I don't feel quite right."

One ritual, unlike those already mentioned, is practiced to improve the power of the baseball bat. It involves sanding the bat until all the varnish is removed, a process requiring several hours of labor, then rubbing rosin into the grain of the bat before finally heating it over a flame. This ritual treatment supposedly increases the distance the ball travels after being struck. Although some North Americans prepare their bats in this fashion it is more popular among Latin Americans. One informant admitted that he was not certain of the effectiveness of the treatment. But, he added, "There may not be a God, but I go to church just the same."

Despite the wide assortment of rituals associated with pitching and hitting, I never observed any ritual related to fielding. In all my 20 interviews only one player, a shortstop with acute fielding problems, reported any ritual even remotely connected to fielding.

Taboo: Mentioning that a no-hitter is in progress and crossing baseball bats are the two most widely observed taboos. It is believed that if the pitcher hears the words "no-hitter" his spell will be broken and the no-hitter lost. As for the crossing of bats, that is sure to bring bad luck; batters are therefore extremely careful not to drop their bats on top of another. Some players elaborate this taboo even further. On one occasion a teammate became quite upset when another player tossed a bat from the batting cage and it came to rest on top of his. Later he explained that the top bat would steal hits from the lower one. For him, then, bats contain a finite number of hits, a kind of baseball "image of limited good." Honus Wagner, a member of baseball's Hall of Fame, believed that each bat was good for only 100 hits and no more. Regardless of the quality of the bat he would discard it after its 100th hit.

Besides observing the traditional taboos just mentioned, players also observe certain personal prohibitions. Personal taboos grow out of exceptionally poor performances, which a player often attributes to some particular behavior or food. During my first season of professional baseball I once ate pancakes before a game in which I struck out four times. Several weeks later I had a repeat performance, again after eating pancakes. The result was a pancake taboo in which from that day on I never ate pancakes during the season. Another personal taboo, born out of similar circumstances, was against holding a baseball during the national anthem.

Taboos are also of many kinds. One athlete was careful never to step on the chalk foul lines or the chalk lines of the batter's box. Another would never put on his cap until the game started and would not wear it at all on the days he did not pitch. Another had a movie taboo in which he refused to watch a movie the day of a game. Often certain uniform numbers become taboo. If a player has a poor spring training or a bad year, he may refuse to wear the same uniform number again. I would not wear double numbers, especially 44 and 22. On several occasions, teammates who were playing poorly requested a change of uniform during the middle of the season. Some players consider it so important that they will wear the wrong size uniform just to avoid a certain number or to obtain a good number.

Again, with respect to fielding, I never saw or heard of any taboos being observed, though of course there were some taboos, like the uniform numbers, that were concerned with overall performance and so included fielding.

Fetishes: These are standard equipment for many baseball players. They include a wide assortment of objects: horsehide covers of old baseballs, coins, bobby pins, protective cups, crucifixes and old bats. Ordinary objects are given this power in a fashion similar to the formation of taboos and rituals. The player during an exceptionally hot batting or pitching streak, especially one in which he has "gotten all the breaks," credits some unusual object, often a new possession, for his good fortune. For example, a player in a slump might find a coin or an odd stone just before he begins a hitting streak. Attributing the improvement in his performance to the new object, it becomes a fetish, embodied with supernatural power. While playing for Spokane, Dodger pitcher Alan Foster forgot his baseball shoes on a road trip and borrowed a pair from a teammate to pitch. That night he pitched a no-hitter and later, needless to say, bought the shoes from his teammate. They became his most prized possession.

Fetishes are taken so seriously by some players that their teammates will not touch them out of fear of offending the owner. I once saw a fight caused by the desecration of a fetish. Before the game, one player stole the fetish, a horsehide baseball cover, out of a teammate's back pocket. The prankster did not return the fetish until after the game, in which the owner of the fetish went hitless, breaking a batting streak. The owner, blaming his inability to hit on the loss of the fetish, lashed out at the thief when the latter tried to return it.

Rube Waddel, an old-time Philadelphia Athletic pitching great, had a hairpin fetish. However, the hairpin he possessed was only powerful as long as he won. Once he lost a game he would look for another hairpin, which had to be found on the street, and he would not pitch until he found another.

The use of fetishes follows the same pattern as ritual and taboo in that they are connected only with hitting or pitching. In nearly all cases the player expressed a specific purpose for carrying a fetish, but never did a player perceive his fetish as having any effect on his fielding.

I have said enough, I think, to show that many of the beliefs and practices of professional baseball players are magical. Any empirical connection between the ritual, taboo and fetishes and the desired event is quite absent. Indeed, in several instances the relationship between the cause and effect, such as eating tuna fish sandwiches to win a ball game, is even more remote than is characteristic of primitive magic. Note, however, that unlike many forms of primitive magic, baseball magic is usually performed to achieve one's own end and not to block someone else's. Hitters do not tap their bats on the plate to hex the pitcher, but to improve their own performance.

Finally, it should be plain that nearly all the magical practices that I participated in, observed or elicited, support Malinowski's hypothesis that magic appears in situations of chance and uncertainty. The large amount of uncertainty in pitching and hitting best explains the elaborate magical practices used for these activities. Conversely, the high success rate in fielding, .975, involving much less uncertainty, offers the best explanation for the absence of magic in this realm.

June 1971

FURTHER READING

Magic, Science and Religion by Bronislaw Malinowski (New York: Doubleday and Company, 1948).

"Water Witching: An Interpretation of a Ritual Pattern in Rural American Community" by Evon Vogt in *Scientific Monthly*, LXXV, 1952, pages 175-186.

Soccer As a
Brazilian Way of Life

JANET LEVER

Soccer in Latin America is more than a game, more than a Saturday afternoon amusement for work-weary fans, more than a means of employment and sometimes high reward for an athletic elite. It is an all-consuming commitment bordering on fanaticism.

In June 1970, El Salvador severed diplomatic relations with its neighbor Honduras over a dispute that erupted during an important soccer match. The first two of the three-game World Cup regional finals were enlivened by riots as the fans from both countries attacked each other on the field. As a result, the final game was played in the shadow of 1,700 riot-ready police who had been called in to guard the stadium. The feelings aroused by the games were intense, and they opened the way for serious grievances between the two countries to surface and explode. Soccer played the role of a catalyst; it was a short leap from the soccer arena to the political arena and El Salvador's decision to shut down diplomatic channels with Honduras.

Elsewhere in Latin America, too, excitement sometimes boils up into mass rioting over nothing more than a single foul. In fact, some stadiums now under construction contain playing fields ringed by moats to prevent crowds from attacking referees or rival teams' players.

Within Latin America the best soccer players and the most dedicated fans are found in Brazil. One demonstration of this came in 1966, when thousands of people from all social classes followed their team to England hoping to celebrate Brazil's third consecutive championship in the World Cup finals. To their profound shock, Brazil was eliminated early in the competition. Back home, Brazilians were grief-stricken. *Time* reported: "From office buildings in Rio and Sao Paulo clouds of black carbon paper and typewriter ribbon cascaded onto the streets below, flags were lowered to half-mast, and people wept in public."

Rio, Sao Paulo and Belo Horizonte, the largest soccer centers of the nation, produce the most extreme Brazilian soccer fans. In these cities soccer assumes such an important place in the fan's life that it may take on a religious fervor, with a man ritually burning candles in his team's colors to summon supernatural support for victory. A recent Sao Paulo study by Antonio Euclides Teixeira produced a particularly telling statistic that indicates the tremendous influence of soccer on the fans:

In the weeks that the Corinthians (the most popular team in the city) win, production in Sao Paulo rises

12.3 percent. In the weeks in which the Corinthians lose, the number of accidents at work increases by 15.3 percent.

So much for the fan, but what happens to the soccer player in a society that carries its sports enthusiasm to such a fever pitch. In America it is practically a cliché that professional sports are a standard means of social mobility for lower-class people who have the prowess to succeed. It might be worthwhile, then, to apply this proposition to Brazilian soccer to discover to what extent, if at all, the game provides a way of "making it."

British sailors visiting the port city of Rio de Janeiro first introduced the sport in 1864. For many years the game was played only by managers and officials of English business establishments in the country and by the Germans in the population who formed their own teams. Eventually these groups were joined by sons of the Brazilian elite who had learned the game while studying or traveling in Europe. This was an era when soccer was "chic," the game being restricted to the few who knew the sport and the few who had access to the aristocratic clubs where it was played. Players were mostly university students who came from the wealthiest families and were preparing for careers in the traditional professions.

It was a number of years before laborers passing the playing fields on their way home from work picked up the game. But from idle spectators, they became eager retrievers and before long they were players in their own newly-formed district clubs.

The lure of the game proved so attractive, in fact, that by 1913, soccer had become the national sport of Brazil. Paralleling its growth in popularity, the technical level of the sport continued to develop. By 1914, Brazil felt ready to test its proficiency against other countries, and competed in its first international match in Argentina. European soccer, meanwhile, became professionalized. Brazil found it had to compete for its own players who were being lured away by attractive offers of fame and fortune. Finally in 1933, Brazil, too, was forced to professionalize. The transition changed the face of Brazilian soccer considerably but not uniformly throughout the nation.

One striking outcome of the professionalization of the game has been a drastic change in the socioeconomic origins of professional players. Rather than become club employees, the players from elite backgrounds immediately quit their soccer careers, their places being taken, by and large, by players from urban middle-class backgrounds. Today, however, more than 80 percent of Brazil's professional soccer players are from the lowest class.

Since what we are talking about here is a total of over 5,000 professional players attached to some 100 teams—an industry, in other words, of considerable importance—one might be excused if he came to the conclusion that soccer in Brazil does indeed provide its lower-class players with (in Daniel Bell's words) a "queer" ladder out of the grim poverty into which most of them are born. That this is not always or even often the case, we shall see. But what we can also see in Brazil is the process by which the sport has developed over time. For soccer is not everywhere professionalized to the same degree, and there are some cities, and some clubs within those cities, where the game is still played as it was at the beginnings of professionalization. Thus by comparing the state of soccer in a small city such as Curitiba with soccer in, say, Rio, one can set up a kind of archeological slice into the history of the sport. This is important to understand soccer as a Brazilian way of life.

In Rio or Sao Paulo the large clubs do a lot more than field their soccer teams. They also function as extremely elaborate social clubs, basically for financial reasons. Soccer alone is not very lucrative, and to sponsor a good team is expensive. A club must pay players, maintain grounds and pay rent to the stadiums that are owned by the state or by large clubs. Professionalism also means paying employees such as coaches, trainers, referees, linesmen, doctors, masseurs, wardrobe men, dieticians and cooks. Only directors serve their clubs without pay, getting instead the honor and sense of satisfaction that comes with contributing to their favorite team's success.

Social clubs, however, can be highly profitable. The major clubs in Rio and Sao Paulo offer so many recreational and other activities that they must keep two completely separate administrative directories, one for the soccer team and the other for the social club.

Rio's Fluminense Club, for example, is considered the most elaborate soccer social center in the world. Its stark white walls roofed with red tile form a compound in one of the central districts of the city. When not watching games at their own football stadium with a 25,000 person capacity, members of this elite club can use a massive gymnasium or wander through well-groomed gardens. In addition they enjoy tennis courts accomodating more than 2,000 spectators, three swimming pools, steam baths, rifle range, a bar and beautiful club buildings which house the administrative offices, library, long trophy galleries, restaurant and ballroom. The Fluminense also offers a host of social activities— dinners, dances, fashion shows, theatre, movies, parades and picnics. There are amateur soccer teams for all age groups, volleyball teams, basketball and salon soccer, bowling, ping-pong and swimming meets.

In soccer's early years a man joined a soccer club simply because he was a fan. Now, as soccer clubs have assumed an important social role, a man may have wholly different motives when he buys his membership. In informal conversations, some Fluminense members even admitted to being fans of the Flamengos, the team fielded by the lower-class club in the city. As one man explained it:

I like Fluminense's facilities for tennis and swimming, and my wife wanted me to join because her friends all gather here in the afternoon for cards. Although I've always loved the Flamengos, their membership is made up of the humble people—we'd have nothing in common, and I certainly wouldn't want my daughter with their sons at any club dance.

The Fluminense was the last professional club in Rio to hire Negro players. Only within the past few years have Negro social members been accepted. It is one of the few clubs in the country that is exclusive also in the sense of a maximum number of members. So selective is this club that an applicant undergoes rigorous screening even after submitting a long personal questionnaire, on which he must divulge not only his present socioeconomic status but his family tree as well. The club's list of ineligibles covers the usual categories—criminals and persons with contagious diseases—but goes a step further to exclude handicapped individuals, excepting those who were maimed while fighting for their country or while in the service of the Fluminense Club. The Fluminense is so restrictive, in fact, that its own players, although worshipped on the field, are treated as "employees" and are prohibited from attending many of the social events, particularly dinners, theatrical performances and most special dances. They may attend minor functions such as picnics and parades.

On the other hand, in Curitiba, a city of 650,000, the five professional soccer clubs also describe players as "employees," but they invite team members to the clubs' social activities. These clubs, though, are a good deal less sophisticated than those in Rio. Although Curitiba clubs would like to develop their social sectors for financial reasons, they still concentrate mainly on sports activities. Because professionalism is less developed in Curitiba, the clubs still retain some of the solidarity of amateurs. This provincialism carries over into salary scales too. The Curitiban player earns much less than the professional in Rio (an average annual salary of $3,000 in Curitiba compared to $5,000 in Rio), and so a fan can still feel that the player is fighting for the love of his "shirt" (the club's uniform), not just for the money.

The salary differences are not all, however; there are additional benefits to playing for one of the big Rio clubs. At the most a Curitiba player may pick up an additional $500 in bonuses, but a player in Rio may add $1,000 to $2,000 to his salary through bonus incentives. Rio players also may receive $5,000 to $15,000 upon signing a contract, while Curitiba players sign on for nothing.

Only two of the five soccer clubs in Curitiba sponsor social activities, and these are the two whose membership is middle class. Curitiba Football Club, founded in 1909, is the oldest club, followed by Agua Verde, which began in 1914 when a group of Italian immigrants broke away from the predominantly German Curitiba Club. Six years later Atlético, a social club for the elite, began to function also as a sport club. In 1933, the railroad company founded its own team, the Ferroviário (meaning "railroad employee"), to boost morale and foster unity among its workers. The last club to enter the professional arena was Primavera, named after the suburb in which it was founded just six years ago.

Unlike the posh Rio clubs, those in Curitiba are generally quartered in rather modest buildings that house membership files, a few meeting rooms and a tiny administrative staff. Behind the clubhouse is the stadium, usually a fairly small one, that also serves the team as a training field. One club, however, has substantial grounds and facilities, and its stadium is being enlarged to accommodate 80,000 fans. A new pool and bowling alleys add to the club's attractions.

It is no accident that this club, Curitiba, is the oldest or that its team is the most professionalized. Generally speaking, the older the club the more it approaches those of the big cities in style. The most recently founded of the city's clubs, Primavera, is still barely more than an amateur district club and has a membership of only about 500. At one time, the clubs could also be distinguished by the social class of their memberships, with the sons of the elite playing and cheering for Atlético while Negro railroad workers fought for the Ferroviário. But over the years, largely because of the pressure to expand their facilities, the clubs' memberships have become much less homogeneous socially and now, for example, Ferroviário has many middle- and upper-class members who joined because of ties to the railroad company or simply because they admired the team. One consequence of this is that because of the great social distance between the two groups of members, and because class snobbery is rife in

Brazil, Ferroviário's directors are certain that the membership would be unreceptive to social activities. As proof, they pointed out that their swimming pool, although most conveniently located, is the least frequented of all the clubs' pools.

Another example is Atlético. Founded as an upper-class club and still referred to as the "Top Hats," Atlético has nonetheless steadily accepted lower-class members to help defer the increasing costs of maintenance. But here again, social mingling becomes impossible. Only Agua Verde and Curitiba, with their relatively homogeneous middle-class memberships, are able to include social as well as athletic activities. The socially mixed clubs in Rio and Sao Paulo, however, and especially the popular clubs, do successfully sponsor social activities. The more open, liberal atmosphere of the large cities perhaps accounts for this.

Be that as it may, Curitiban clubs, lacking developed social activities, must pursue financial survival by methods very different from those of the clubs in Rio and Sao Paulo. No soccer club in Curitiba is as selective as the Fluminense. A Curitiban applicant need only list his name, dependents, address and occupation and pay an entrance fee proportionate to the benefits of membership. A lifetime membership in Curitiba costs 500 cruzeiros ($160), as compared to 1,000 cruzeiros ($320) for some Rio clubs.

The high entrance fee in the larger cities is only one reason why these clubs can be highly competitive for players and their teams highly professional in performance. Their memberships are also much larger; some Sao Paulo clubs average 100,000 members, compared to 10,000 in Curitiba. Because of their huge followings and the greater capacity of their stadiums, large clubs often receive enough income from the gate to maintain their teams. In addition, the Rio and Sao Paulo clubs can count on substantial public relations donations from commercial interests and tax concessions from the state governments, which receive revenue from the rental of public stadiums. The stadiums in Curitiba belong to the individual soccer clubs.

A common fund-raising device in Curitiba is to sponsor a "promotion" or a membership drive in which temporary memberships are offered for small monthly payments or in which takers get the chance to win a car raffle with the purchase of inexpensive temporary memberships. Atlético and Curitiba make money by bringing famous teams, such as the Hungarian national all-stars or the Royal Madrid champions, to Curitiba for special games.

The least professionalized club has the most trouble meeting its maintenance costs. Primavera has only 500 members and the revenue from the gate is negligible, since the young club has not yet developed the kind of traditional rivalries that attract large and loyal crowds. Because it must keep its expenses at a minimum, Primavera can only pay its athletes $50 per month while Curitiba and Atlético both offer $160.

At first glance it might seem that Primavera would have to be content with inferior players, but this is not the case. The real difference is in the recruitment methods used by clubs of varying economic power. The Primavera cannot afford to entice good, established players with $1,000 bonuses, nor can it risk disqualification from the special division by hiring less skilled players. The solution lies in contracting new, inexperienced players who demonstrate high potential during informal suburban games or in amateur district matches.

These boys are so grateful just for the opportunity to launch professional careers that there is no question of a bonus.

In order to find such youths, scouts for various teams scour the beaches of coastal towns and the lots and playing fields of the inland cities in the hope of signing some barefoot hard-driving boys who appear loaded with potential and who with a little luck and rigorous training may become stars. Soccer-playing begins very young in Brazil; one often sees four- and five-year-olds using small rubber balls to mimic their older brothers. By the time a boy is in his early teens, he is conscious that soccer might be his road to success, and many play as though they felt the eyes of the scouts boring into their backs.

There are also, in Brazil, the equivalent of little leagues, where many middle-class boys spend hours on the soccer field perfecting their skills. But it is the poor boys, perhaps, who in the tradition of the rags-to-riches American sports story, most desperately want to make it to the "juvenile teams" and then on to pro status. Too poor to afford soccer balls, these youths will practice the whole day through on beaches or empty lots with only tightly rolled stockings for a ball.

Signing these players is far from a cheap venture for the team. That is, most of them are extremely poor and they have long suffered from an improper diet. Before sending them into a professional match, the club dieticians must fill them with needed foods and vitamins; the trainer must rebuild their physiques and the dentist must fix their teeth. Most importantly, the coach must teach them that the game they have played so adeptly since early childhood has intricate rules that every professional must master. Even if the training is successful, the club has no guarantee that its investment will produce returns. Often the player who was quite good as an amateur cannot get used to the crowds of spectators that professional games draw. Some simply crack under the pressure of being paid to win for such a demanding audience. Worse yet, a poor boy from a rural slum might not be able to adjust to city life. Drawing a salary for the first time, he may overindulge in various pleasures: throwing wild parties, drinking too much, dining too late. All these factors can lead to a very brief professional career indeed.

On the other hand, many amateurs do succeed in the professional sports world. Some even become idols, both in the smaller cities and in the big time with big clubs. Although the older, wealthier clubs occasionally recruit in the "sticks" where the poor live, most often they choose not to risk their resources this way. They don't have to. They can let clubs such as Primavera do their scouting and training for them and then raid the smaller clubs for their best players, a practice that is fairly profitable for the smaller clubs as well. In Brazil, not only does the player receive money for signing a new contract, but the club he leaves also receives payment for selling the old contract. Primavera makes a profit by selling off its successful new players.

But what of the soccer player himself and the relationship between his career and moving up in his society? My information derives from a series of 40 semistructured interviews with players and directors from diverse professional clubs in Rio, Sao Paulo and Curitiba and from biographical material on players past and present. From the evidence, I concluded that soccer provided a better route of mobility during the game's early stages of professionalism than it does now. On the surface, the highly professional player from Rio or Sao Paulo who earns almost double the salary of the Curitiban player, would seem to be in a better position to move up the social ladder. In reality the opposite seems to be true; this is due to the lack of long-range stability in the big glamorous clubs.

Many uneducated, poor boys in Brazil rise quickly as professional players for the big clubs but many also lose their footing and fall almost as rapidly and as far as they came. The less professionalized clubs, however, help their players achieve social advances that are enduring, if not always as steep. The responsibilities of professionalism that come with higher salaries in the big cities also close the doors on opportunities for advancement in the athlete's postplaying career. Rio and Sao Paulo teams require daily training as well as something called *concentration*, which means that for four or five days before each game the player is restricted to the club grounds so that the director can monitor his eating and sleeping and be sure that he abstains from sex. An important side-effect, however, is that the big city soccer player cannot hold an extra job. His salary makes another job unnecessary of course, but the point is that he is effectively cut off from the world of long-term careers and this is dangerous for his future.

All players must be literate. While for many this means they can barely read and write, there are some Brazilian players who would like to go to school for vocational training. Professional soccer, however, leaves no time for classes. Student players are nonexistent in Rio and Sao Paulo, although Curitiba averages four university students per club. A mere 20 years ago, 90 percent of all players in Curitiba were students, and 40 years ago the same was true for Rio and Sao Paulo. The number of student players decreases yearly as a club demands more and more time of its players.

Between the student players and the fully professional soccer players are the athletes who hold part-time jobs. Most clubs in Curitiba are at this intermediate stage; the players still have both the time and the need to work. For example, one director of the Ferroviário Football Club reported that of the 30 players on the team, 17 have other jobs. In Brazil, as in the rest of Latin America, men commonly hold two or three jobs, the salary from one usually being insufficient. The small city club thus raises the player's standard of living not only by paying him a professional wage but also by helping him secure a second job, often a better one than ordinarily would have been within his reach. Of the 17 working players in Ferroviário, ten are employed by the railroad company itself, which automatically provides a job to any player who wants one. This job secures the player's economic future far more than does his temporary and unpredictable career in sports. And the player who is able to finance his studies with the money he earns in soccer also achieves lasting social elevation through the sport. Four of the six student players interviewed said they couldn't continue their schooling were it not for the money they earned in soccer.

The possibility for stable social advancement through soccer also exists in the larger cities, but it is elusive. The intelligent player, realizing that his soccer career is only temporary, spends his money wisely and invests his savings. Unfortunately, few players do this. For the majority, soccer provides only fleeting social mobility, leaving their educational levels and values unchanged. Many, inexperienced at budgeting their funds, squander their money faster than they earn it on fancy clothes, sports cars and expensive trips. Around the age of 30 they find themselves with no work skills, no money and only memories of their brief careers. Professionalism has greatly reduced soccer as a stepping stone to a more permanent career.

So far I have not discussed another major characteristic of Brazilian soccer, the "star" system—*estrelismo* in Portugese—which the Brazilians have carried to lengths unknown even in American sports. Pele, for instance, is the world's highest paid athlete ($341,000 per year). He has even been honored by having a street and a candy bar named for him.

Stardom on this scale is only possible, of course, in the big city clubs that have the resources to pay for it. And the system works well enough in terms of greater payoffs at the gate. But soccer is a team sport par excellence and the star system often shatters a team's solidarity. Rivalry goes beyond mere glory. The bonus system in Rio and Sao Paulo, depending on individual achievements, puts a wide gulf between the salaries that teammates receive. In Curitiba the players of one club receive equal bonuses and any differences in salary are due to length of service to the team. The players remain unified in a common goal, depending upon one another for their living. Also, the turnover rate within the team is minimized. In the highly developed soccer centers, the composition of a team can change entirely over a two-year period (one reason being that no second chances are offered after a bad season), whereas in Curitiba teams remain fairly stable for as long as five years, enough time to build strong loyalties among players that the big teams lack.

Heitor, a goalie who was loaned by a popular Sao

Paulo club to Agua Verde for a year, commented on the vast difference between playing in a big center and playing in Curitiba:

> The behavior of one player for his teammates is an attitude of friendship—it's like a family here. In Sao Paulo, it's different. There they are stars. They think they alone were responsible for the victory. The only player who can win a game by himself is Pele—and he's the most humble of all of them. He shows consideration and even love for his teammates. Here in Curitiba, there are no stars—only the "shirt" is important.

Clubs and spectators both are responsible for the scene-stealing side shows that stars often put on to enhance their own prestige. A player may try to score from a ridiculous vantage point rather than pass to a fellow player who is in a better position to score. Stars are not made by passing. The bonus and the applause go to the man who scores, not the person who set up the play. The good of the team is also often jeopardized by such stars in that they will risk personal injury in order to make a grandstand play, thereby risking the success of the entire team. Such activities take their toll.

At the end of their careers, each new generation of soccer stars experiences a terrible depression, a phenomenon naturally related to the punishing professionalism they have been subjected to—a combination of economic and social isolation and the psychological distortions inherent in stardom. A star's adjustment to ordinary life is extremely difficult. The professional begins his career at the age of 17, often earlier, and usually retires between the ages of 26 and 30. Because he neither studied nor worked during his playing career, a lower-class retiring player has no choice but to accept a menial, unskilled job, which is hardly commensurate either with newly acquired middle-class tastes or the symptoms of stardom. Even if a player could adjust to his new salary, change his spending patterns and eventually pay off his debts, he would still find it very difficult to accept the oblivion imposed upon him by fickle fans.

Once a player's legs begin failing him or his reflexes are no longer what they had been, or if his game suffers from skipping training, most often he tumbles from the glories of packed stadiums back to the obscurity he came from. Unless the player was within the ranks of the *estrelismo,* there is little chance the fans will seriously wonder what became of him once his name is erased from the score card. When his playing days are over, people assume the soccer player goes back to his home and applies himself to some skill he acquired before he was discovered. But for most, the only skill they ever had was soccer.

There are, however, players who distinguish themselves in various occupations after leaving the game. Everyone can rattle off the names of such-and-such a player who now owns a chain of sporting good stores or so-and-so who became a coach. Sometimes a player may be placed by an influential director into a government agency as a low-level clerk, and although the fans will never know what became of him, he at least has a job. But many times, players from poverty-stricken environments return to the slums, picking up what they can.

The most famous example of such a case is that of Garrincha. A mulatto slum boy who played his way to the top and made it to two World Cup series with Pele in 1962 and 1966, he plummeted into obscurity shortly after the 1966 series. A deft player, extremely popular during his playing years, he was found jobless some time later, living in a Sao Paulo slum with his wife and nine children. Some extreme cases of maladjustment end in suicide. Rumor has it that four of five deaths of ex-players in the past decade were actually suicides. In the case of Maneco, a Negro player in Rio, there was no doubt that his suicide stemmed directly from his declining career. Maneco's friend and teammate, Leonidas, explained the suicide and said that hearing of the death was the saddest moment of his own career:

Maneco couldn't get a job. The money he received from soccer was going down because he couldn't play as well any more. He just gave up. He was behind in his rent and was evicted. So he committed suicide—over a $20 debt. The club should have helped him, I thought, but it didn't.

Leonidas' own story is typical. He was a very popular Negro player who made the leap from sandlot games to a professional career in Rio at the age of 14. Both he and his wife are from very poor families. The son of a telegraph line watcher, he never received any education as a boy. Like Pele and all other poor Brazilian boys, the focus of all his life's dreams was on a soccer career. Leonidas realized his dream and played until the age of 33. Retired from sports now, he lives in a small shack with his wife and seven children in Curitiba, his home town.

Suprisingly, however, Leonidas is not bitter. He is grateful that his soccer career secured for him a low-paying job as a public functionary and he insists that without soccer he would have become only a bricklayer's assistant, a most humble job. Besides, he pointed out, he enjoyed tremendous prestige during his career and even played on tour in Europe, a part of the world he wouldn't have known otherwise.

In contrast to Leonidas, there is Caju, a professional player who decided to remain in Curitiba despite tempting offers from Rio and Sao Paulo clubs. Reportedly the best Brazilian goalie of the thirties, Caju proudly displays telegrams he received from big city clubs offering fabulous bonuses if he would leave Curitiba and play for them. He refused them all, he explains, in order to keep his job, realizing that he would have no time to build a post-soccer career in either of those cities. His club in Curitiba arranged a part-time job with the public health department, and he is now chief administrator. Even when the clubs do not arrange jobs, an ex-player in a small city can rely on the many influential acquaintances he made socially during his career to secure him a good position.

Thus, in Curitiba, ex-players usually escape the adjustment problems of the players in Rio and Sao Paulo. Having never become "stars" like the players from the larger soccer centers, they never experience that break with reality common to stardom. In addition, they usually avoid the economic crises faced by the big professionals. Many studied while playing football, preparing themselves for new careers or, like Caju, they worked part time, usually continuing in the same jobs full time after retirement. For these men a real continuity exists between life and sport.

But, as professionalism takes hold, the problems of the player in Curitiba will undoubtedly approach those of Rio and Sao Paulo athletes. The level of expertise in Curitiban soccer is rising, and the game appears to be going the same route it took in the big cities. All of the clubs, except Primavera, have now adopted the system of concentration, although in Curitiba the confinement lasts at most only one or two days prior to a game. Still the number of club training sessions in Curitiba is now up to four afternoons per week.

The higher his salary, the greater are the player's responsibilities to his club and to the public, and the less time he has for his personal development. This deeper sense of obligation is the great difference between the very professional and the semiprofessional athlete. Because he is paid to win, the professional feels more like an employee as the degree of professionalism increases. As Paul Weiss commented in his book *Sport: A Philsophic Inquiry:*

A professional athlete must produce pleasure in the spectators and profit for his employers. . . . The professional is a workman, an employee. . . . Money has been invested in him. He is property, whose primary role is to repay that investment.

The careers of Brazilian soccer players do not lend support to the typically American notion that professional sports offer easy routes of mobility for their players. The differences between the Brazilian and the American cases are as important as the similarities. For example, soccer is the *only* sport Brazilians play professionally, which makes it a more significant route of mobility than any single sport in America. Moreover, Brazil has no soccer "season." The game is played year round. The consequences of this difference are crucial, for in the United States a professional player can train for his future profession and resume his normal identity during the off season. He thereby sidesteps the social disorganization that plagues the retired Brazilian player.

Recruitment patterns in America and Brazil are also different. Whereas in Brazil scouts search the beaches and the outskirts for talent, the American professional athlete is often discovered on his university team. In fact, many good athletes enter universities that would have been financially or academically out of their reach had it not been for their athletic prowess. The American athlete, then, starts from a better socioeconomic position and is initially much better trained for a post-sports career. For him, the more professionalized the sport, the better are his chances for enduring social advancement. Not so for the Brazilian athlete. Rather, the least professionalized clubs often help their players up the social ladder while the most developed clubs see their players make tremendous improvements in their standards of living, only to find that their new social roles are as temporary as their playing careers.

It is certain, at any rate, that any ladder of mobility such as professional sports takes on a much greater significance in a traditional, rigidly stratified society such as Brazil than in a relatively open social system such as in the United States.

December 1969

FURTHER READING

"Crime As An American Way of Life," in *The End of Ideology,* by Daniel Bell, The Free Press of Glencoe, 1960.

O Negro no Futebol Brasileiro by Mario Filho, (Rio de Janeiro: Editora Civilizacao Brasileira, S.A., 1964).

"Mengo, tu e o Maior," *Realidade,* Ano II, No. 14 (May, 1967).

Gol de Letra—O Futebol na Literatura Brasileira by Milton Pedrosa, (Rio De Janeiro: Livraria Editora Gol, 1968).

"A Isto Se Chama Religiao," *Realidade,* by Antonio Euclides Teixeira, Ano II, No. 15, (July 1967).

A Historia do Futebol Carioca: 1905-1960, Rio de Janeiro, by Adolpho Schermann, 1960.

Part Three

THE CONTROL OF PLAY
VS.
PLAY AS CONTROL

Classical Music
and the Status Game

JOSEPH BENSMAN

The classical musician dealing with the layman alternates between exhibitionism and embarrassment at being regarded as a freak. Both feelings stem from the same cause—he is ill at ease with the "civilian population." He can most easily relate to them by showing esoteric knowledge of his craft. Like the psychiatrist, the astronaut, the atomic scientist or any other professional in a world of specialists whose work is inaccessible to others, the classical musician finds that the role he plays with laymen is almost always his professional one.

Discomfort with outsiders and the desire to seek out others like himself is often typical of the member of what Max Weber called a "status community." Such a community is composed of people who make adherence to a certain complex of values and practices the organizing principle of their lives. The professional musician, for example, having made his choice of a career, has committed himself to the relative superiority of the value of music and musical pursuits.

Musicians tend to concentrate their social contacts on those who have chosen the same way of life. Many of them draw their friends almost exclusively from fellow professionals or devoted amateurs. They frequently marry other musicians and raise children who become seriously interested in music. They entertain each other—playing for pleasure when not performing, rehearsing or practicing professionally. They frequently attend concerts or listen to records or FM radio. Many of them have their own students to whom they transmit the tastes and values of the musical community as well as their own technical expertise.

Their social contacts with nonmusicians are usually limited to family members and old friends from their premusical days. Contacts with neighbors, officials and the rest of the "civilian population" are necessary but minimal. The musician may, however, have a nonmusical hobby—such as gardening, painting or craftsmanship in household repairs—in which he takes particular delight as proof of his nonprofessional humanity. (The reverse situation frequently is found among other types of professional people, such as doctors or engineers, who may cultivate music as evidence of their broader interests.)

The musician, then, lives very much within the confines of his status community. Such communities have in fact replaced the territorial communities of earlier times as the fundamental units of society. The modern city dweller organizes his life around his vocation or profession, his clubs and voluntary organizations, his hobbies and leisure-time activities—not around the physical limits of his block or borough. The geographical limits that used to constitute local or "natural" boundaries have become irrelevant, and people have formed psychological communities in their place. The New York musician is more at home in the concert halls of Salzburg, Moscow and London than in the apartment of his next-door neighbor.

A vast number of these status communities exist in urban society. Each is based on a relatively narrow set of values, internally consistent but often in conflict with those of rival communities. Taken together they present an enormous array of life styles for the city dweller to choose from.

It is precisely because of these often unrelated ad hoc status communities that the breakdown of a simple overall societal structure does not result in widespread social and personal disorganization. People organize their lives around the office, the club or the union, confining their contacts to people with similar interests and thus preventing themselves from having to deal with an apparent infinity of social relations. The complexity of the metropolitan culture lies in the number of its diverse status communities, and not necessarily in complexity of life for particular individuals. Many people are so firmly encased in their own status communities that they are effectively isolated from the kaleidoscopic urban life going on around them. The professional musician, for example, may not know how the stock market is doing, who is running for city councilman in his district, or exactly why the workers at a plant he passes every day are on strike. Furthermore, he may not care.

How do these status communities develop and gain a recognized place in the social order? This process is closely related to the formation of status-giving audiences. The status-giving audience for professional musicians consists partly of their fellow musicians, but most of its members are laymen. This group serves as the ultimate validator of the professional's claims to status. It confers prestige by accepting his claims to prestige. Its members join the opera guild, support the symphony drive, attend concerts and buy recordings. In doing so, they implicitly affirm that the musician's product is a valuable one, and that its producer is entitled to certain recognition.

This prestige system operates the other way as well. In allying themselves with the musical performer and accepting their emphasis on aesthetic values, the lay members of the classical music audience borrow a certain amount of prestige from their performing idols. They are recognized in their own circles of acquaintance as people with knowledge of and taste in the arts. As lovers of classical music, they bear society's official badge of cultivation. They adopt the whole gamut of symbols, culture, speech, dress and consumption styles that become characteristic of a status-giving audience. This process perhaps goes furthest and is most evident among the teenage audience that grants prestige and support to pop musicians, but there are elements of it among the classical music audience as well.

What are the characteristics of the status community that classical music lovers support? Relative isolation from the rest of the world combined with the relative density of social relationships within the musical community results in a rather inbred culture. What is it like, and what does it take to be admitted?

First, it takes years to become thoroughly familiar with the technology, skills, rhetoric and technical symbolic systems upon which music is based. This knowledge is necessary for full-fledged entry into the musical community.

Further, it takes years to assimilate the folklore of this farflung group. Most professional musicians know hundreds of others. Taken together, they have moved through a great variety of musical organizations and have intimate knowledge of the people and events associated with each. This common experience—the source of countless anecdotes and endless speculation on the talents and careers of other performers—provides even previously unacquainted musicians with a solid basis for conversation. It is through such networks of personal interchange that, for example, a member of the New York Philharmonic may have a working knowledge of the Cleveland Orchestra, the London Philharmonic, the Philadelphia Orchestra or the Vienna or Berlin Philharmonic, as well as of the soloists who perform with these orchestras. This is why the musical community in London may be closer and more familiar to the New York musician than the events in his immediate neighborhood.

Through his union, or guild, the musician has a vast fund of technical information related to his salary and modes of payment. He is alert to special legal arrangements in this area. He wants to know about the organization that pays his salary, the hours, wages, vacations, rehearsal time and pay, and about the financial arrangements which make these possible. If he plays the tympani in a symphony orchestra he finds out not only the approximate fee he will receive in a similar group, but what he can expect performing in the pit during a Broadway musical.

A string player may object to the salaries paid the

woodwind, the brass or tympani players, since theirs are
substantially higher per note than his own. These latter
musicians feel that they deserve the higher pay, however, since they tend to play more solos and participate
more in smaller intraorchestral ensembles, where mistakes are more noticeable. They believe they should be
paid for quality, not quantity.

Some instrumentalists appear to be able to bargain
more effectively than others as individuals. They are
paid far above the minimum scale.

Musicians' major institutional enemies are conductors
and critics. The performances of individual conductors
always provoke comment. The conductor who can't
maintain a beat, who loses his place, who "hams it up,"
who abuses his orchestra or a particular instrumentalist,
or who loses control of his orchestra or of his temper
will be the source of countless anecdotes that circulate
through the international music community.

The musician regards the conductor as an arbitrary, capricious martinet whose knowledge of music is
eclipsed by his egotism, megalomania and flair for
histrionics—qualities he can indulge to the fullest when
he ascends the podium.

The nature of the conductor's position invites these
responses, for the conductor is required to control,
direct and discipline simultaneously, in a public setting,
as many as a hundred or more specialists, each of whom
in his own specialty feels he is more competent than the
conductor. Each will resent the discipline to which he is
subjected, especially if it is administered unskillfully.

The instrumentalists tend to feel that the conductor
gets the credit for a good performance, the performers
the blame for a bad one. The conductor, of course, is
better paid and is a celebrity. Thus the musician often

perceives him as a social climber and a traitor to the art of music.

The conductor, on the other hand, is likely to feel that his instrumentalists are lazy, incompetent and obstreperous. He may regard them as children who resist the discipline necessary to create an ensemble. If a firm hand is not used, he may reason, they can wreck the orchestra and destroy his own reputation. Both conductors and instrumentalists can cite instances of this having occurred.

Another institutional enemy of the musician is the critic. He is more the enemy of the soloist than of the orchestra member, but both regard him with caution. Whether or not they respect his judgment, they must respect his power. He has vast influence over the lay audience; he can wreck the career of a soloist, a conductor or an entire orchestra. Musicians regard him as arbitrary and capricious to the extent they think, as they sometimes do, that he is bent on destroying a performer, conductor or ensemble. Such professional paranoia is least common among members of the orchestra because they see each review as part of a campaign, with the cumulative effects being greater than a single battle. To the soloist, however, a bad and possibly unjust review or one based on an "off night" can be a Waterloo.

Musicians often view critics as frustrated performers whose failure as musicians has led them to merely talk and write about music and to compensate for their own inadequacies by attacking those musicians who have not given up. The musician sees criticism as an act of resentment against creation and creators. Nevertheless, the critic's opinions will be warmly applauded when he castigates the work of a rival performer or group.

The critic is usually considered superior to the music historian or musicologist, unless the latter happens to be working on specific problems of performance or on unearthing valuable lost manuscripts.

Major performing groups (and likely individual performers) select one or more special rivals almost in the way that college football teams do. For the rivalry to be meaningful, the two contestants must be almost equally matched. Each performer or performing group has distinctive characteristics which form the basis for competitive evaluations, both favorable and unfavorable.

Thus, regardless of the music played, the Philadelphia Orchestra is viewed either as having the richest singing tones in its string section—or as being overblown, overcolored and excessively romantic.

The New York Philharmonic is regarded as a source of great individual performers—or as a collection of disruptive individualists who are often underrehearsed, overperformed, and directed by too many different (and not always competent) conductors, all of whom they seem bent on destroying.

The Cleveland Orchestra is viewed by other musicians as being one of the most disciplined groups in the world, but one whose tempos often exceed the score or the intentions of the composer.

The Boston Symphony is sometimes viewed as the most balanced orchestra, and occasionally as a most dull and academic one.

Among soloists, similar distinctions are made. Some are known for tone (and oversentimentalizing the music); others for virtuosity (and playing too fast, loud and inaccurately). Some are authentic (and too cold and academic); others are poetic (and too mannered or personal in their styles).

These stereotypes suggest that there is a great deal of categorical thinking within the musical community. It is so large and its culture so varied that some sort of pecking order is necessary for identification and placement. How do musicians divide up their world and assign their fellows to more or less prestigious pigeon-holes?

Conductors, soloists and opera stars are at the pinnacle of the prestige structure. This is true for conductors despite the institutional hostility that performers have for them. Stars and soloists derive their prestige partly from the unique skills and personal qualities that convert a highly talented professional into a star. There appears to be relatively little envy of great performers by able performers who are not stars.

Among soloists, size of fee is likely to help determine prestige. Victory in such competitions as the Leventritt, Chopin or Tchaikowsky music festivals bestows prestige, as well as the possibility of performing fees sufficient to sustain a successful career. Ownership of a valued instrument—a Stradivarius, Guarnieri or Amati—confers prestige on the string player.

Conductors, soloists, ensembles, composers and even critics and musicologists may receive prestige by the type of music they are identified with. One conductor's reputation may rest on his advocacy and interpretation of new or experimental music. Another may be known as the foremost conductor of Beethoven, Mahler or French Impressionist music. The same applies to soloists and smaller ensembles. A soloist or ensemble may revive a previously forgotten master such as Alkan or Telemann or rank as the foremost interpreter of a composer, style or composition. Ensembles may specialize in Baroque or Renaissance music or in minor works by great masters. Some critics are able to write more intelligently or knowingly than others about a particular composer. A musicologist or a critic may be responsible for resurrecting a forgotten mode, and a composer may similarly adapt a neglected style.

If the musician, as lobbyist, succeeds in establishing a reputation for such specialization or leadership in stylistic movements, he acquires the prestige of the musical style, composer or type of music, often independently of his own technical or performing skill.

Prestige is also based on the type of performing group. In general, small permanent ensembles such as trios and string quartets bestow more prestige to their members than larger ensembles. We might regard this as an extension of the prestige continuum of the soloist, the conductor and the star. Anonymity, in the sense of being lost in the welter of sound created by a large performing group, diminishes prestige. The rating of "share-of-total" performance intersects with the rating of the performing group.

The great American symphony orchestras have high prestige, as do about a dozen chamber groups. Rivalries about the exact prestige ratings of these ensembles operate at all levels.

Types of instruments are also a basis of prestige. The strings and piano are high prestige instruments, followed generally by the woodwinds (especially the oboe), with lower prestige assigned to the brasses and percussion. Within these instrumental groups, desk or chair is important, and the position of concertmaster is highly prestigious.

Age is important both with respect to position in the

orchestra and the prominence of the soloist. The musician who achieves a high position at an uncommonly early age receives special prestige. The child prodigy, for example, has unusual opportunities in music. Likewise, since musical performance also involves physical skills and equipment that deteriorate as the performer ages, unusual prestige accrues to individuals who retain their performing skills long after the age of expected decline.

Recording opportunities are also a source of prestige for both the soloist and the ensemble. Within the symphony orchestra, recordings are frequently played by less than the full orchestra. An invitation to perform as a member of the reduced orchestra (the "Mozart Orchestra," for example) or as a soloist within the ensemble is a prestigeful event.

Accompanists have lower prestige than featured performers. This includes orchestral accompaniment of a ballet, opera or musical, as well as of a soloist. But the prestige of the accompanist is directly related to that of the soloist. An accompanist to an outstanding soloist may have even higher prestige than a soloist of middle rank.

With some exceptions, music teachers have relatively low rank. The teacher who is also a performer receives the prestige of his performing role (which helps him in recruiting top students) and not of his teaching role. The teacher of soloists and outstanding performers receives part of the prestige of his students. The teacher affiliated with a conservatory or music school receives the prestige of the school (if he has no higher source of prestige). The student or aspiring soloist will receive prestige from affiliation with a teacher of high rank and distinction.

The teacher who does nothing but teach and who has

not previously made a reputation as a performer is the low man on the prestige scale. This is a source of anxiety and chagrin to music teachers' guilds, as well as a reason for their existence.

We suspect the composer's prestige (except that of well-known "star" composers) depends more on who performs his work and how he makes a living than on his function as a writer of music or the particular qualities of his compositions.

The many-sided quality of prestige within the musical community reflects its division into smaller subcommunities, each of which is highly specialized and has its own internal system of prestige. Sopranos, bassoonists and percussion experts all have their own criteria of excellence for ranking the members of their own specialties.

Moreover, every type of musical expression has its own culture. This is true because the individual musician moves from organization to organization within the same type, and music fans frequently attach themselves to a particular genre, such as chamber music or the opera.

Some musical communities are entirely separated from the groups described above. Folk, popular, jazz and ethnic music are each the basis of separate status communities which have their distinctive cultures and systems of social honor. The classical musician is usually a layman in his relationship to these other musical communities.

In a society consisting of many and varied status communities, each community will have its stars, its own special elite. The mass media makes celebrities out of these stars, making them visible not only to the people of their own group but to each other and to the public at large. These celebrities then form a super-elite.

A labor leader who can halt the routine functioning of a vast segment of the economy by calling a strike becomes a public personality. In the same way a temperamental opera star or a piano virtuoso becomes visible outside the community of music lovers through television reportage, guest appearances at civic events and news and gossip coverage in the national and international press. An orchestra conductor or a comedian may become a social lion, the friend of kings, queens and presidents.

All the traditional ways of ascribing status—wealth, education, talent, ethnic background, family background and the rest—become of secondary importance to stardom, leadership, elitehood. The heads of wealthy old families entertain and are entertained by society prostitutes, ex-junk dealers, former bootleggers, band leaders, ethnic politicians and Hollywood film personalities. If they are stars in their own status areas, the sons of immigrants and the descendants of slaves can become social equals with the traditional upper classes.

A massive trading of social status takes place within such a system. The parvenu movie idol or sports hero or political figure starts to receive invitations from members of the old upper classes. They can offer him a certain social legitimacy to go with his new wealth and power. But he can offer them something too: the rewards of publicity and recognition, and the feeling —not to be underestimated in a society geared to the image of the jet set of being "where the action is."

This sort of mutual social backscratching among the leaders of different status communities is what binds their communities together in a workable system of exchange. And it is just this star system that provides a

basis for pluralism without anarchy. Musicians trade
status with labor leaders, painters with politicians and
professors with presidents, but each is still firmly
anchored in his own status group.

As part of this exchange, the very wealthy serve on
the boards of various specialized institutions. They
contribute financial support to these organizations as
well as lending the prestige, influence and authority of
their respective spheres of prominence. In return they
receive social recognition and personal satisfaction.
Entertainers assist in fund raising by guest appearances,
by allowing their names to be used, and by appearing as
officers in voluntary organizations whose major purposes lie outside their special field. In politics the status
community leader becomes an important source for
dramatizing support for a candidate, issue or policy.

The coordination, integration or coalescence of the
elite communities is by no means perfect or complete,
however. There is no single super-elite, no unity of all
status and power leadership. The vast complexity of
urban society prevents such unity. The number of status
communities that produce candidates for the super-elite
is too large. As a result, there remain many different
elites and many different combinations or alliances into
which they may fall. The exchange system works, but
not with the precision or the predictability of a finely
tuned machine.

A huge number of more or less temporary alliances or
subcommunities exist among the elites. They are not
organized in any specific or formal way, but depend on
the mutual selection of various stars and leaders. These
subcommunities may have overlapping memberships.
Some may be based on membership in only a few status
communities; others will be drawn from different value

and institutional spheres. An individual may be a member of a number of subcommunities, and be excluded for personal or other reasons from others.

Some will be organized for specific purposes—to support a given organization, policy or person—and may dissolve or change membership and character in a relatively short period of time. They may compete for attention, may divide on major issues or may be unrelated to each other.

As a result, it would be difficult to support the charge that the elite community is an organized, unified conspiracy. Individual elite subcommunities may, of course, be organized for specific purposes and therefore appear to contain elements of a "conspiracy." But their purposes are often purely social or cultural. They appear to be a conspiracy because they are temporary alliances of "men at the top" which exclude men at the middle or the bottom from all roles but those of complying or serving. Resentment is natural and human.

These patterns of organization among the elite subcommunities explain in part how it is possible to coordinate a society so complex that most of its members can live in only one or a few of a vast number of status groups.

I have concentrated on sketching the inner workings of one such group—the classical music community—to give a closer look at one of the many building blocks of the prestige system in a competitive mass society.

September 1967

Audiences—and
All That Jazz

RICHARD A. PETERSON

Nat Hentoff, prominent jazz critic, asserts that "Jazz is one of the few vocations that allows a man to be himself, to say in his work who he is and what he feels." Jazz shares this characteristic with the other creative arts. However, the picture is not so idyllic for artists; the old adage still holds true: "He who pays the piper calls the tune." In order to make a living the musician is often asked to play what he considers the antithesis of jazz—commercial, popular, corny, sweet, square's music.

The relationship between an occupation and its clientele is a central concern of the sociology of occupations. The position of artists, just as jazz musicians, is particularly interesting because the artist's claim to competence is not buttressed by the trappings of a professional organization or the titles of an established bureaucracy or the elaborate rules of the craftsman's guild. The musician himself must defend his conception

178

of jazz as an art form against the commercialization of recording companies and the "vulgar" taste of the audience. The pressures for compromise are heavy. For example, Jimmy McPartland recalls an incident with a recording company executive in which Benny Goodman, Glenn Miller and Tommy Dorsey were also involved:

After the (recording) session was just about over, we started kidding around and playing corny. Out comes the recording manager from his booth, and he says, "That's it! That's what we want, just what you're playing there." We were playing as corny as possible. As a matter of fact, Tommy Dorsey had come up and was standing listening to us, and he picked up a trombone and started playing, kidding around, too. The manager said, "You gotta do that." That is what he wanted. So we sort of used the *St. Louis* chord progressions and blew all this cod Dixie, and we called the number *Shirt Tail Stomp*. It sold more than any of the others; or I should say that it sold the rest of the sides because it was corny. It shows the taste of people; still the same, I guess, the world over.

A performer can pander to the tastes of his audience or he can ignore them. He can try to educate the audience to raise its standards, or he can reject audience standards altogether. Jazz musicians have tried out all these possiblities at one time or another, as they search for an attitude that can preserve their self-image as creative artists without putting them permanently on the unemployed list. However, as we shall see, none of these strategies provide a final resolution of the audience "problem."

A complete acceptance of audience standards can produce a Lawrence Welk, whose musical philosophy is "to play music not so much what we enjoy as what people in general enjoy." Welk, of course, does not really have the jazzman's problem. He sees himself as an entertainer rather than as an artist, and is content to have it so. Jazz musicians feel that complete surrender to audience taste will destroy their creative abilities and recount with horror stories about those of their fellows who have "gone commercial." Jazz artists are fated to some form of battle with the audience.

In nightclubs and dance halls where jazz is most often played, the artist's contact with the public is quite intimate. Here jazz musicians feel they must defend themselves and their music from the audiences' corrupting taste. They try to ignore the audience by construct-

In nightclubs and dance halls where jazz is most often played, the artist's contact with the public is quite intimate. Here jazz musicians feel they must defend themselves and their music from the audiences' corrupting taste. They try to ignore the audience by constructing what Kenny Dorham, a trumpet player, calls " 'the fourth wall.' . . . You're aware of the audience and yet you have to preserve a sense of detachment so you can create a piece of music or a role internally." They develop a system of communication through the music which is shared among the musicians " . . . like an inside joke." They "put down" the audience in innumerable ways, in the music, through jokes and antics and through not honoring "requests" from the audience.

The audience cannot be ignored entirely, of course. Musicians are performers, and performers are not paid to entertain each other. The players employ other tactics to cope with the audience.

One possibility is to educate the audience to want to

hear good jazz and to respect the jazz artist. This education can be open, working through the schools as Stan Kenton and representatives of the musicians' union have advocated. Alternatively, it can be disguised education, jazz smuggled into dance or commercial music. This is the strategy most often advocated by practicing musicians and also the one which is most readily available to them. The late Jack Teagarden put it most simply. " . . . You just can't go out there and play every number fast to show off your technique. You've got to play some numbers for the dancers . . . play four tunes for the public and one for yourself." Gene Krupa shows this disguised education strategy to be the conscious intent of the swing era Benny Goodman band. "Benny built himself a band playing musicians's music, but didn't shoot over the heads of the public. It took the people time, but once they grasped the Goodman musical sermon, they easily understood, accepted, and followed." The commercialized jazz of Dave Brubeck and Stan Kenton has been excused by some critics as whetting the appetite or preparing the audience for true jazz.

The basic problem inherent in diluting creativity to educate the audience is that jazz is ever changing. Today's excitingly creative jazz is tomorrow's commercial pap. Thus, inevitably, the audience is being educated to *yesterday's* jazz. The forty-year-old lady who knows enough to yell for "Saints" doesn't know that this tune and the style which it represents had been thoroughly explored as an art form before she left grammar school. The half-educated audience asks the artist to produce again and again the things that have made him famous. This can have a devastating impact on the artist's career. As Andre Hodeir, French jazz historian, tells the story, "the history of both jazz and jazzmen is that of creative purity gradually corrupted by success. . . . First, the young musician expresses himself freely, breaks the rules, disconcerting and even shocking his listeners; then the public adopts him, he attracts disciples and becomes a star. He thinks he is free, but he has become a prisoner."

Rather than diluting the jazz elements, the music may be made palatable to the audience by occasional gimmicks. In the twenties this strategy was given the name "nut" jazz. Here jazz virtuosity is exaggerated out of all proportions and built into a routine. While some jazz historians have claimed that the gimmicks of Cab Calloway and the personality of Louis Armstrong sustained jazz through the thirties, such exhibitionism is strongly resented by race-conscious artists today. The clowning of "nut" jazz has come to be associated with debasing Negro stereotypes, and the aloof stage manner of the "cool" jazz musician is a deliberate attempt to repudiate this association. As the paragon of the cool manner, Miles Davis says, "All I am is a trumpet player. I only can do one thing—play my horn—and that's what's at the bottom of the whole mess. I ain't no entertainer, and I ain't trying to be one. I am one thing, a musician."

Attempts to bring the art of jazz to the audience—either by diluting it or putting it in an amusing package—result in a stifling of creative artistry. There is one alternative remaining, total rejection of the audience and its standards. It's a very short jump for most jazz musicians from the rejection of lay evaluations of music to the development of a special jazz community which rejects the standards of society in the rest of life as well. The jazz musician begins to see all the world outside the jazz community as essentially hostile. The jazz community cuts itself adrift from the rest of society. In this isolated community the cult of creative genius and the fierce competitiveness of jazz artistry have led to the use of all sorts of artificial means (alcohol, drugs, magical devices and the like) to heighten sensitivity to the art and to dull the consciousness of an alien audience. Thus, jazz community demands may bring the musician to destroy himself. Fabled cases of self-destruction for the sake of art are those of Bix Biederbecke and Charlie Parker.

The final irony in attempting to get free of audience demands through bohemianism is that the audience comes to expect and demand outré behavior. The would-be audience-alienator is asked to go on with his "show." What is intended as a rejection is converted into a new brand of entertainment, a new style, reminiscent of nut jazz. A recent note in *Down Beat* magazine concerning one of the most innovative modern jazz artists illustrates this point well:

> Charles Mingus, often discussed as a petulant stormy petrel, is often more victim of the news-conscious than he is really two-gun notorious. Witness his last engagement at New York's Village Gate. Co-owner Joe Tremini called Mingus' manager to demand some action. "What's going on?" he asked the manager. "Mingus has been here for a week now; no trouble; no telling the customers off. Talk to Mingus, will you? It is bad for business."

September 1964

The Dance Studio—
Style Without Sex

HELENA ZNANIECKI LOPATA
and
JOSEPH R. NOEL

The ballroom dance studio is a business organization teaching adult students the skills utilized in the "polite companionship" activity of social dancing. As a training school it technically performs the same function as a ballet studio or a business college teaching typing and shorthand. Unlike those groups, however, the ballroom dance studio has been subject to "exposés" by information media, lawsuits by allegedly victimized persons and negative side smiles by society at large.

A reference to such an organization usually provokes numerous insinuations of sub-rosa activities or "shady" relations and indignant cries of "exploitation." Taking ballet dancing lessons for years wins societal praise; taking ballroom dance lessons for years labels one a fool. Studios, whether independent or organized into national chains are aware of the "scandal bugaboo." The structure of studios—as well as the social roles and relationships within them—is deeply influenced by all this criticism and by the ideology developed to justify their existence.

Americans view a business firm catering to the public as a "secondary system" with depersonalized, utilitarian, goal-oriented relations whose members are "out to make a buck" through all the legally permitted techniques which lack personal and "empathetic" interests in the recipient. The customer supposedly enters these centers to obtain a specific service, independent of personal feelings about the personnel. "Primary relations," on the other hand, are viewed as involving affection, personality-directed goals, pleasure in the relationship itself and trust in its symmetry or reciprocity. Partners in a primary relationship are expected to commit themselves to equal involvement and to be concerned over each other's feelings. The presence of commercial lonely hearts clubs and ballroom dance studios violates this distinction since they supposedly attract defenseless people who want primary relations so badly that they are willing to use secondarily designed organizations to buy them.

In our society, one of the forms of interaction in primary relations with members of the opposite sex—friends, dates or loved ones—is ballroom dancing. An important factor distinguishing this form of interaction from others—such as bridge-playing or simple conversation—is the fact that it involves physical contact and psychological concentration or attention on the part of a man and a woman who are supposedly attractive to each other, although it takes place in the presence of other couples engaged in similar activities. Its sexual connotations are implicit in the attitude of members of the society toward two women who dance together and the refusal of men to dance with each other.

Ballroom dancing involves much more than the skill of knowing how to move legs and body to musical rhythms. It is a complex system of interaction between the two partners and between the couple and the others on or near the dance floor. People in American society assume that people who frequently dance with each other in ballroom situations are personally important to, and concerned with, each other and therefore have a strong influence upon each other. The fact that a commercial establishment may be used to teach such a skill in situations purposely modeled after a "polite companionship" scene leads to assumptions of insincerity, inequality of involvement and fraud, and to indignant judgments of the cost of such learning as being equivalent to a "fleecing."

Interestingly enough, the societal picture of a student enrolled in courses of a ballroom dance studio and the studio's image of the same student are similar, although producing different evaluations. The society sees the student body as composed of rich but lonely older women and unsocialized or inadequately socialized young adults. The studio sees the student as a lonely person who needs the interaction provided by its activities, and who needs the skills to be used to facilitate increased participation in events on the outside. The assumption that the student is in the studio because of his inability to relate to people in a satisfactory manner thus conforms to the ideas of both viewers.

The similarity of sketches ends there—the society sees the student as gaining nothing but a fleecing and it is very suspicious of the undue influence of "gigolo" teachers upon these lonely and unsophisticated, but rich, old women and young adults. It defines long-range courses of instruction as the use of life savings to buy primary relations which are dishonestly pretended. The studio sees itself as providing important services, increasing the person's self-confidence and poise, and teaching him, or her, to relate to others in new ways, in addition to providing fun for persons who do not have much of it in their lives. The ideology of the studio thus stresses multileveled help to students who are unhappy without it. Neither image stresses skill in dancing.

The ballroom dance studio is designed in its training of teachers, organization of "events," physical appointments and intertwining of student-teacher relations to teach a complex of skills and knowledge. These connect persons in temporary interactions—but do not unite them into any total social relationship. This specialized training is part of a person's developing knowledge about how to conduct himself in society.

The basic function of teaching a child the details of demeanor and the forms of deference—how he and others should move, talk, dress, approach others and accept recognition—is carried on by family and peer groups. Ballroom dancing is one of the social skills that may be "picked up" by teenagers from their friends or through formal classes conducted by a professional teacher.

Ballroom dance masters are known to have existed in Europe for several centuries prior to the formation of studios. They came to the homes of upper-class families not only to teach dance steps but as arbiters of etiquette; they were viewed as essential for both the social instruction of the young members of the household and to keep the older members adequately up-to-date in social etiquette and behavior. When dance studios began to appear in Europe in the latter part of the eighteenth century they still undertook the teaching of etiquette in addition to, or as part of, the teaching of dancing. It was their aim to teach primarily young upper-class members. The nineteenth century saw an expansion of the number of studios in America.

The shift in dancing, from groups of couples joined into a common circle doing the same movements, to single couples forming closed circles with increased body contact, resulted in great changes in the significance and form of the dance, in the methods of teaching and in the attitude of society toward it. Dancing came to be seen as a very personal activity to be engaged in by persons who are in "appropriate" relations of polite companionship.

A second major change in the significance of dancing is a result of changing class patterns in America. Upper-class members have taken some of the training previously given the young at home into outside forms of education. Dancing has also been taken over by the youth of all social classes and by adults of the middle class.

Since the ability to interact in dancing is considered one of the skills required of members, or aspiring members, of the upper classes, but knowledge of its methods is often insufficiently available, the dance studio exists to fill the gap. That is its basic function. The learning of "the etiquette of dancing" can, however, be a very expensive venture. Lessons at chain schools cost between $5 and $9 per half-hour or $10 to $18 for the standard one hour. Thus, an introductory course of 30 hours costs the student anywhere between $300 and $540. Most studios attempt to enroll students for at least 100 hours for $1,000-$1,800 but, as several well-publicized lawsuits have pointed out, women have been known to sign up for lessons totaling more than $10,000.

Many ballroom dance studios in America are franchised components of national or regional chains and bear a chain name. The two largest chains were founded and named after professional dancers with the implication that the student will reach similar proficiency as he learns their techniques. The national office and the various regional suboffices arrange for the advertising of a consistent image, for the training of teachers, and especially for various contests. Regional dance directors help train new teachers, add the glamor of far-away places, increase identification with the system, and help to insure the maintenance of standards in order to counteract or prevent negative images created by the behavior of individual studios. Sales contests, rewarding teachers for selling the greatest number of future lessons with prizes of cash or trips to glamorous settings, and dancing contests which draw teams of one student and one teacher from member branches provide an external focus of activity.

Each studio has a manager, responsible for its maintenance; for advertisement synchronized to that of the larger areas, yet appropriate to potential local clientele; for the development and functioning of control systems upon primary relations with students and for the assignment of duties and rights. His staff may consist of a studio dance director, a guest director, and a receptionist. The studio dance director has three major obligations:

☐ to teach potential teachers, or "trainees"

☐ to provide dance instruction to novices and to regular teachers

☐ to keep dance material current through contact with regional and/or national dance directors.

He is also the instructor in the "Trophy Club," a voluntary association of advanced students who utilize studio facilities to hold meetings in which dancing is the principal activity and who go out to public places as a group.

The "guest director's" function is to encourage students, teachers and trainees to bring guests to the studio to witness lessons in progress or to participate in "parties" which are regular or special events, usually held on Friday evenings, duplicating social occasions on the outside. These guests are an important source of new students, and the parties are used to bring them into the studio in order to provide opportunities for signing them up for courses.

The teaching segment of the studio is divided into two branches—the "junior consultants" and the "teachers." The consultants form the front department of a studio and have the function of converting a potential student into an actual one within what is called a "dance analysis" of eight private lessons of half an hour each, usually combined into four one-hour sessions, plus a varying number of practice sessions and parties. If he is successful (we shall refer to all teachers, in front or back departments, by the masculine pronoun and all students by the feminine although the reverse is as frequent) the student is signed up for a certain number of lessons in a specified course and turned over to a teacher. The teacher's function is not only to teach the student to dance, according to the outlined schedule, but to insure "renewals" for large blocks of lessons or possibly even for life-time courses.

The front department is headed by a senior consultant whose main function is to enroll a newcomer into the contract or agreement of courses, with the cooperation of the junior consultant. He is the main interviewer and salesman. The teachers work under a supervisor who assigns students, supervises the planning of courses and assists in renewal sales. The supervisor draws up the agreement after the teacher has designed a course plan.

The ballroom dance studios in America have developed a complex and rather standardized set of techniques by which to convert a potential student into an actual one and to insure continued lesson-taking on her part. The system is dependent, in the beginning especially, upon the development of primary relations between the student and the teacher, within, however, the controls of their respective roles. In the long run, the primary features of relation must be decreased and shifted to the studio and its personnel in general, since teachers have a rather short period of membership in any one studio. Some of the best students may outlast most of the teachers. The aim of insuring the continued presence of students permeates the whole behavior system of the studio, from the training of the teacher to the comments of the receptionist. The teacher's patterned relations with all other members of the studio are focused upon the development in him of the ability to teach dancing in such a way as to make the student happy—keep the student willing to continue being taught.

The physical appearance of many studios is generally designed to give off an aura of "class," meaning upper class. It is dignified, impressive, plush and yet "comfortable." The reception room and the ballroom are particularly impressive, the latter resembling a hotel ballroom.

According to the studio image, the new student is very nervous and bashful. This expectation is undoubtedly realistic as a stranger who enters a smooth-running and formal-looking establishment is usually nervous.

The average prospect doesn't actually want to start coming to the studio. After all, most people don't *want* to take lessons in anything—learning sounds too much like hard work. Besides, most people are embarrassed about taking dance lessons. They are afraid that their family and friends will laugh at them. So there are two strikes against taking lessons before the prospect even enters the reception room. *(From an instructors manual.)*

The prospect had visualized, according to staff expectations, that she could "brush up" for about $10 to $25. The two consultants must convince her to enroll for a longer course. As a training manual points out, "To someone who expects to learn to dance in a few hours and to spend not more than about $25, the 100, 200, and 400-hour courses come as a shock." The new student often does not accept the idea of a long-range plan and the senior settles for a minimum of four hours of lessons. The most frequent aim is to obtain enough hours so that the junior has time to extend the original starting course. "The most important thing is to get the person started taking lessons," states the manual.

The "best teachers" in the studio are assigned to this function, and a shift from back to front department is a promotion. Actually, it is not only the dancing ability but also the selling ability of the teacher which is needed for such placement. The front department teachers tend to be the best looking and smoothest but their teaching technique, as the manual explains, is completely different from that of the back department teachers. The front is seen as the department which helps the prospect, in spite of her ignorance, to commit herself to enough lessons to cover a long course. The junior must speed-teach superficially without allowing the student to feel that she knows all there is to know and therefore needs no more lessons.

The junior convinces the student that dancing is a pleasurable activity with the use of several specified techniques including frequent positive or complimentary comments about the ability of the student and her areas of improvement. Some of these comments are recorded in the course plan which contains a running record and is used not only to organize each lesson but as a visual proof of improvement. The junior is encouraged to write such statements as:

Worked on timing, Miss Jones in good mood today, so very relaxed. Covered footwork in F.T. [fox trot] No. 3, Rumba Side Break A for Intro. & Change of weight in Lindy. Miss Jones is a lot of fun.

The demand for personal comments, especially for compliments, on the part of the temporary speed teacher and later, on the part of the regular teacher is based on the assumption that the student deeply needs primary relations. Without them, the assumption goes, she will not continue to learn, which would entail a loss not only to the studio, but to her. The March 19, 1965 story in the *Chicago Sun-Times* devoted to the widow who is suing the Arthur Murray dance studio for

$150,000 reinforces the importance of these primary behavior patterns of the studio staff. The suit charged that, not only had the studio taken "advantage of the fact that she was a lonely woman . . . " and convinced her to buy $58,899 of dance lessons but that she "quit the club . . . after employees of the studio had become 'cool toward her.' "

The junior constantly reminds the new student that theirs is a temporary relation and that soon she will move on to a regular teacher. The staff has assigned the pupil to a teacher, and a point is made of introducing them to each other before the end of the fourth hour. The emphasis upon "the transition" to a regular teacher shows some concern that the student might become too dependent upon the first person with whom she spent so much time and enjoyed herself. The junior must be free to take on, and convince, new students.

The student and her chart move on to the regular or "back" department. The teacher has been prepared for this contact by training not only in dance patterns and in the teaching of these, but in the handling of pupils. In one of the studio chains, for example, he is told that there are three basic categories of students to be handled differently:

☐ *Pure dominants* who are described as logical decision makers
☐ *Compensatory dominants* who are seen as not assured or confident but aggressive and difficult (The teacher is advised to let both dominant types feel that they are controlling the situation or voluntarily agreeing to each stage of it, and not to respond to the compensatory dominants in a negative way.)
☐ *Submissives* who require sympathy, sincerity and a

confident control, as they suffer from an inferiority complex.

The daily pattern of life in each studio is usually similar. The full-time teachers come into the studio at about 1:00 P.M. for afternoon appointments or in order to be available for new students. They usually continue till 9:30 or 10 in the evening. The teacher checks the receptionist's books, which chart the appointments for that day. He goes to the teacher's room to obtain the course plan or chart for the first student. When the bell rings or, if he is bucking for a sale or promotion, just before the bell rings, he walks into the reception room with "front-stage" demeanor to "pick up his student on time." Students must not be kept waiting for the teacher since such a delay can easily be interpreted as a lack of interest.

The interaction with the student begins when he "lets her know how glad he is to see her." The greeting is supposed to be buoyant and accompanied by both a smile and a compliment. Teachers are instructed to look for something new about the pupil—a dress or hair style. Comments about this have the function of forcing the teacher to really pay attention to each student as he approaches her and to make her aware of his personal attention. The same routine is repeated every day with every student.

The lesson itself is supposed to follow a pattern interweaving informal interaction and formal instruction. The teacher must do the opposite of the junior consultant. He must teach slowly, but thoroughly. The student, having been convinced by the front department that she can learn to dance very rapidly, must be made to realize that the process of learning is slow, without being discouraged.

The glamorous setting of the ballroom, the presence of other dancers, the chart, mirrors along one wall, the atmosphere of *fun,* and the romantic undertone— combined with the desire of the student for such a setting and primary relations—lead almost inevitably to the growth of dependence. The lessons take one hour, which is a long time for a tête-à-tête. They usually occur two or three times a week and involve a great deal of personal interplay in conversation. If a teacher is good at his task, he is able to constantly shift between instruction, suggestion which is not strong enough to be criticism, compliment, dancing and polite conversation.

The dependency of the system upon the primary relations developed by the teacher with the student can best be seen in the directions for insuring "renewals." Long before the present course expires, the student is prepared for the need for more lessons. By now she has been to the studio frequently, for lessons or attending one or more parties, and has become acclimated to its atmosphere. One of the methods utilized to encourage her increasing involvement with the teacher and the studio is a trophy examination.

The trophy system unites the teacher and the student and gives them a goal or purpose. It contributes to the renewal system which is the life line of the studio. These contests are used as one of the arguments to influence the student to renew, on the assumption that she will be interested in helping him to win it.

Formerly, the largest block of lessons which a student could purchase was the "life-time course." The manual lists 12 types of people "who would like to be Life-Time Members," including the persons who "would like to have a social calendar of better than 50 social events per year planned for their enjoyment and know

that they will have these for the balance of their lives."
A typical list of events the person gets with the life-time
course indicates the social life schedule of the studio.
Besides the lessons—at discount and with 25 hours of
private instruction free—she will have:

Four special, fun-filled Life-Time parties per year,
free; attendance at all technique or class sessions,
free; attendance at all Trophy Balls, free; membership
in the Life-Time Club; executive membership in the
Trophy Club; free attendance at any and all student
functions sponsored by any . . . studio anywhere in
the world.

A Life-Time program could cost $10,000 in one of
the chains, and the studio states that it loses money; this
claim is based on the assumption that the person who
buys it will take advantage of most of its affairs for
many years.

Recently, studios have tended to replace these "life-
time courses" with similar, shorter-range packages even
including trips to glamorous vacation lands. One of the
functions of the package programs is to shift the
dependence of the student upon her particular teacher
to involvement with a studio and through it, with the
whole chain of studios. Both teachers and single studios
tend to have relatively short life cycles, but the national
organizations insure that this will not result in extra law
suits by allowing lessons purchased on any of the
multiple-hour plans to be taken at any of its branches.

There are controls to prevent any relations between
student and teacher outside the studio. Studio rules
about this are very definitely stated in chain manuals,
and many teachers have been fired for breaking them
and even blackballed so they could not obtain another
job within the organization. The basic rule states that:

It is absolutely forbidden for any studio employee to go out with any pupil or ex-pupil at any time other than a studio-supervised function and then only with the express consent of management; and in this instance the employee will not meet the pupil before the function in order to be escorted there or will the pupil be allowed to escort the employee home.

The studio rules even include an explanation for it:

Experience has shown that deviation from this rule creates poor control of the pupil and in many instances has wiped out the good reputation of a studio.

Further, the first series of lessons, given by the junior consultant, are held within small, private rooms, because of the assumption that the prospect is too uncomfortable about the whole experience and too bashful to try dancing in the large, formal and busy ballroom. Female juniors are trained to handle a "fresh" student—to discourage sexual advances and concentrate his attention on dancing. Both they and male teachers are further protected by the fact that each of the junior rooms has an interoffice communication system with nonconcealed speakers and a window in the entrance door, enabling anyone going by to glance in.

The regular teacher teaches in the ballroom. The formality and upper-class appearance of this room discourages lower-class comments or implications about the relation. The presence of other teams of students and teachers and the accessibility of the room decrease the intimacy of the physical contact of the dance. The constant training of teachers stresses that they must look and act as "gentlemen and ladies." The total atmosphere attempts to be controlled and dignified, without involving sexual or deeply personal feelings.

A third form of control upon the primary relations between teacher and student is purposely used by the studio. Each teacher is encouraged to build up the image of other members of the studio in the eyes of the student and to use them for the exchange of dance partners during lessons and parties. He introduces her to others, shows great courtesy to the students of fellow teachers and reminds his own students that they must learn not only to dance with him, but with other men. The ideology of the studio, in fact, demands that the teacher "transition" a student, that is, prepare her to be shifted to a different teacher. Ideally such a transition should occur about every 100 hours and is explained as necessary for the student's own good.

The secondary reasons for the relation between the student and the teacher also operate to control primary relations. The teacher must teach and "look good" to management. He has several students, and the process of teaching is physically exhausting. He is a paid employee. The student has paid for dance lessons and must justify her participation in the organization by learning. And, whatever the original components involved in the decision to enter the studio, the student can end up wanting to dance well.

Thus, although the students tend to be relation-oriented at the beginning, increasing participation leads them to become competitively skill-oriented. The studio management is aware of this fact and is probably quite right in stating that the long-term courses are most likely to produce the best students—not only in terms of money, but in justifying the studio, and maintaining the rationale. One of the characteristics of the "professionally" oriented studios which separates them from taxi-dance halls or other organizations less oriented

toward skill and upper-class behavior is the "backstage" support of the ideology. In the teachers' room, the inner sanctum in which the controls of posture and language are relaxed, there are no derogatory or degrading remarks about the activity of ballroom dance teaching. Nor are teachers self-deprecating about their task. The regular or "long-course" student who dances well is a source of pride, even in the back regions.

The highly professional studio hires only advanced teachers or trains them carefully, enforces the rules forbidding outside, nonstudio sponsored contact, demands nonsexual connotations in the student-teacher relations and has a noncynical attitude toward dancing and toward the student. It tends to be "back department" oriented with a high morale and strong skill orientation on the part of teachers.

Some fly-by-night studios depend on a fast turnover of many anonymously viewed students who are pressured to sign up for long-term contracts which are often not kept. The grapevine which operates among dance teachers and other studio personnel evaluates studios on their level of ethics, with the standard of enforcement of "relations outside" as an important criterion. Some managers do not enforce this rule, permitting relations among teachers and students which are external to the roles within the studio.

The factors which affect the degree of stress upon learning and skill within the studio include:

□ the influence and control of a national chain demanding maintenance of standards

□ the attitude of management toward qualifications by which it hires and behavior it demands

□ the location of the studio and its dependence upon the "walk-in" student

□ the skill orientation of the personnel and the support-ive ideology it uses as the foundation for behavior
□ the balance between the sources of income between long-range and short-range courses.

In any of its varied forms, the ballroom dance studio is a complex social system in which primary features become a part of secondary roles and in which increased contact may actually increase the secondary features of social interaction.

January/February 1967

FURTHER READING

Presentation of Self in Everyday Life by Erving Goffman, Garden City, New York: A Doubleday Anchor Original, 1959.

Social Roles and Social Relations by Florian Znaniecki, San Francisco: Chandler Publishing Company, 1965.

Social Dance, A Short History by A. H. Franks, London: Routledge and Kagan, 1963.

The Private Lives
of Public Museums

CESAR GRAÑA

Why should a tradesman or a farmer be called upon to pay for the support of a place which was intended only for the amusement of the curious or the rich, and not for the benefit or instruction of the poor?"

William Cobbett in the House of Commons, 1833

By at least two practical and symbolic standards, American art museums are institutions of the highest spiritual and civic pedigree. In monetary societies, freedom from the taint of gain is, curiously, a mark of virtue, and museums as "nonprofit" organizations are, like churches or educational establishments, part of the preserve of "pure" values within the social order. As harbors of such chastity and loftiness, the state in return grants museums an accolade which, though fiscal in itself, declares them to be, like schools and sacred houses, temples of the society's better self: Museums are tax-exempt.

They are, then, not only noble places but public ones. In a democratic nation, however, "public" stands for more than merely "nonprivate." It refers also to a mystical link between the institution and the society, and the society's past and future. The standing of relics and art as part of what the past has entrusted, for all time, to the present has been argued in this country since the foundation of the great storehouses of art and history. Two models of the American museum as an instrument of communal life were born of this argument.

There is first what I will call the *Boston position*. It is patrician and classicist. It believes that works of art should be allowed the full, undisturbed majesty of their meaning, that this meaning should be communicated as a personal experience to those capable of hearing the call, and that, therefore, every man must work his own salvation at the feet of beauty.

The second may be called, with some license, the *New York position*. It is democratic and uplifting. It holds that museums should aid—perhaps seduce—the visitor into a proper understanding of what he is looking at. It believes that art should be ordered, labelled and interpreted, so that in the words of one writer, cultural digestion for the greatest number might be facilitated.

In the early days of the Boston Museum of Fine Arts, Matthew S. Pinchard and Benjamin Gilman, respectively vice-president and secretary of that institution, spoke for the first of these views.

A museum of art, ultimately and in its widest possible activity, illustrates *one* attitude towards *life*. It contains only objects which reflect clearly or dimly, the beauty and magnificence to which life has attained *in past times*. The fruits of this exalted and

transcendant life are gathered within its walls, and it
is the standard of this life with the noble intellectual
activity it presupposes, that a museum offers *for
acceptance by its visitors* [italics mine].

Mayor Cobb of Boston, addressing the audience at the
museum's opening in 1876, also argued for the natural
radiance of art and its capacity to strike and light up the
sensibilities of the citizenry:

All classes of our people will derive benefit and
pleasure from *barely looking* upon objects that appeal
to the sense of the beautiful [italics mine].

However, Luigi de Palma Cesnola, the first director of
the Metropolitan Museum of Art, spoke quite a different language. In 1887 he said that museums should
affect, not only art and the experience of art, but "the
manners and the virtue, the comfort and the wealth of
our beloved people." Two years later, George Brown
Goode, assistant secretary of the Smithsonian Institution, announced that "the museum of the past must be
set aside, reconstructed, transformed from a cemetery
of bric-a-brac into a nursery of living thoughts." And in
1909, John Carlton Dana, a librarian who organized the
Newark Museum Association, drew what may have been
the most literal psychological and social lesson from
Goode's words, stating that museums should be organized as to help the community "to become *happier,*
wiser and more *effective*" [italics in the original].

There are, besides, the voices of social scientists who,
at a recent international gathering, spoke of museums as
institutions dedicated to preserving the peculiarities of
particular places while exalting and diffusing "cultural
values" generally, and which, as spiritual centers of the
community, contributed both to its enlightenment and
its cohesion.

Museums, then, have ideologies. Some of them have been solemn, elegant, "elitist"; others evangelistically democratic or piously utilitarian. Yet, from the social scientists above, one might conclude that museum-going is one of the rituals left to a secular, post-traditional civilization. These contentions and disparities, however, will become understandable if we look into the fabric of ambiguity and paradox which lies behind museums and their history.

Public museums are one of the newer creations of Western culture; with few exceptions they had their beginning at the close of the eighteenth century or, in the great majority of cases, after the turn of the nineteenth. In spite of this newness, however, they are among the most widespread of modern institutions. In the United States and Canada alone there are about 5,000 of them. New ones are constantly being established, and attendance figures reveal a genuine "mass" phenomenon.*

There is no question also that museums will continue to flourish, nursed as they are by some of the contradictory trends of our culture. The destruction of local traditions and the assault upon "the past" perpetrated by industrialization and world-wide modernization seem to make large numbers of people susceptible to an appetite for rules of pre-industrial life. This

---

*On the basis of a partial survey, 127 million people visited museums in the United States. According to the American Association of Museums the term "museum" includes, besides places we can conventionally call by that name, historical houses, historical libraries, planetariums, aquariums and botanical and zoological gardens. Even within the latitude of such a definition, this means that attendance at art and historical museums is, as all known figures indicate, in the tens of millions.

appetite is so intense that it accounts in part for one of the major and most characteristically modern industries: tourism. The most ambitious monuments of earlier life-styles, such as the stately homes of England, or even whole nations, like the prototypically picturesque Spain, have now been reduced to the condition of *objets d' art*. "In the family" events, like the bullfight or royal pageantry, whose mystique was once accessible only to the natives, are now marketed to foreign visitors by the well organized bureaucracies of popularized cultural romance, both private and governmental—that is to say, travel agencies, tourist bureaus, and even tourist ministries.

Museums, then, express modern ambivalences, even dilemmas. In a very real sense the past can be preserved only when it is overrun by the present. And it *must* be preserved because, we are told, the past is a trust—an *inheritance* left to the present which fortifies and guides us in our future tasks. Museums, therefore, must arouse emotions of homage, but not subservience to the ancestral. Piety for history should not be so engrossing or so yielding that it would keep us from moving forward. In a society like the United States, so committed to novelty and to change, this can create some peculiar predicaments. Arthur C. Parker's *Manual of the History of Museums* in 1914 spoke of them as places designed to awaken "feelings of reverence and gratitude" toward the past. He advised, however, that they be kept from accumulating what he called "mental dust."

This elusive but real tension between past and present, which museums induce by their very nature, is made more perplexing by the character of the past they preserve. Museums are public, first because the state has assumed the guardianship of our artistic inheritance, and second because safekeeping these heirlooms is a way of making them available to all. It remains a fact, however, that many of the possessions which art museums so jealously guard are monuments to a past splendor which is inseparable from great names, great houses, great dynasties, great titles, great wealth and great power, a splendor frequently reflected in the subject matter of the works themselves, no less than in their Veblenian significance as instruments for the sumptuary glorification of certain social ranks. On the one hand, therefore, art museums offer to the public a panoply of relics which they claim to conserve as a public heritage. On the other hand they compel our imaginations to turn toward the aristocratic past from which museums often derive their treasure-house magic and their special atmosphere of awe and worshipful respect.

This is so inescapable a conflict within the character of art museums, that, unless we understood it, we could not grasp the significance of the changes which styles of museum display have undergone.

There are perhaps three historical steps in the "staging" of museum collections. If one looks at portraits of eighteenth century aristocrats as they survey their personal artistic possessions, at engravings of the first public viewings of the Louvre, at McKenzie's painting of The National Gallery of London in 1820, or even at photographs of the early Metropolitan Museum, one notices at once a common feature: In all of these the walls appear covered with paintings hung frame to frame, sometimes quite literally from floor to ceiling. The atmosphere is that of a storehouse or a counting-room. The point of view is that of the patron and proprietor. What we see is the *exhibition,* the spectacle of treasures which the public is allowed to invade and marvel at.

Later, as the "religion of beauty" and the cult of personal genius created by the doctrines of romanticism began to take hold, the ordering principle came to be dictated by what may be called the *rights of the artist.* The works of one man were now hung together, and the walls were cleared so that different pieces might stand as particular creative achievements allowing the visitor to enter into single and personal communion with them. The final outcome of this is perhaps to be found in the aesthetic chapels of certain famous museums in which a work, like the *Nightwatch* at the Rijks Museum in Amsterdam, or the *Meninas* by Velázquez at the Prado, is housed in a particular niche or room of its own and made the focus of carefully if not theatrically contrived contemplation.

The concept of the public, however, remained a severely limited one. In their early days, museums like the British screened the "curious and the studious" to see who among them were "proper to be admitted." And the visitors themselves were what would now be called self-selected persons who, by virtue of the cultivation attendant to their class and upbringing, constituted the "natural" audience of art. Today museums must also be considered by the way in which they view their responsibility to the public. The director of one of the most conservative institutions in Europe (and one of the three or four best known art museums in the world) told me that his public duties consisted of keeping the paintings in good condition and opening the doors in the morning. He realized that many people would leave the premises as unknowing and untouched as when they came in. But that was their affair, if not indeed their fault.

At the same time the spread of the democratic principle has created among many museum professionals a sense of larger obligations, a determination to embrace the public, to nurse its sensitivity, and to mediate between it and the work of art. Such spirit of "community service" has always been very strong in the United States, and American museums, with their film series, lecture programs, gallery talks, children's wings and contributing memberships, have become the model for younger European administrators and curators who decry the "antiquarianism" and cultural "royalism" of their own institutions.

Yet, even in the egalitarian United States certain implications of the art museum's princely heritage cannot be avoided. For example, it is a routine task at one of New York's most famous collections—privately endowed but open free to the public—to meet the frequent demands of the school system for student visits. Such requests are accommodated to every pos sible extent, although the director feels that some control over numbers and guidance must be exercised to assure that the visit becomes something more than a tumultuous outing and an empty experience. Besides, the gallery must also be concerned with the informed visitor, who comes knowing what he wants to see and expects to enjoy it with some degree of serenity. What is particularly poignant, however, is the silent discrepancy between the visiting school children, coming as they do from varying social classes and ancestries, and the symbolic world which they find in this famous house of art—superb baronial wood panelling, great ornamental clocks, marble fireplaces, ducal chairs crowned with ancient crests, portraits of noble Britons, and an archetypal gentleman's library stocked with Gibbon, Meredith, Carlyle, Thomas Hardy and Vasari. Inevitably one is left to wonder about the meaning of the encounter. For as they pursue their exposure to art, the children of polyglot New York also find themselves, however tenuously, the guests of a mansion conceived, not only as a monument to "values," but as a reenactment of the patrician past.

Such tension between the external, "democratic" function of art museums and their more secluded internal traditions appears in at least two forms: between museum functionaries and their public clientele, and between museum objects and their viewers.

It has been said that aristocratic patronage in the past schooled writers and artists in the cultivation of "pure" values—that is to say, values which were above any measurable and obvious social *usefulness*. And further, that with the passing of the actual aristocracy, these value-makers and value-keepers (the "intellectuals") were left as the new (and only remaining) aristocracy. Applying this to the modern art museum (whose function is literally that of custodian of spiritual artifacts) one would say that, while museum men earn their *social* position by discharging a public function, they gain their sense of *self-esteem* from their fellow experts and from the self-satisfactions of their own scholarship and expertise.

Whether every museum man is equally sensitive to the integrity of his own separate status must be at this point a matter of speculation. Nevertheless, the issue dominates a great deal of the discussion and self-searching now going on among museum administrators in Europe, where the strain of democratic cultural expectations is beginning to show its effect. Some European directors regard "gallery talks," films and other such "services" as a compromise with scholarship. On the other hand, the British Museum (in the words of its present head) recently described itself as wishing to give "delight and instruction to the widest possible public." It is just as true, however, if indeed not more so, that the British Museum remains dedicated to the academic interests of its research staff. And the impression is hard to escape that, like the great English universities, the British still lives in the aftermath of a convention which brought together two forms of leisure, the scholarly and the gentlemanly. One is, therefore, not surprised to hear that the museum is sometimes challenged to become more concerned with its function as a servant of public culture, and less so with the intellectual passions of the scholarly few.

A Dutch art historian, the director of a famous museum in Amsterdam, agreed that museums might be regarded as educational institutions but never, as he put it with some fervor, as instruments of entertainment. To believe the "keeper" of public relations at one of the most distinguished museums in Great Britain, many museum officials of that country view the public with what could only be described as hatred (though, for obvious reasons, they were careful not to show it). And according to a former museum director, now a functionary of the federal government in this country, the struggle between the roles of educational democrat and cultural aristocrat is a real one, even in the United States.

The question—intellectual self-sufficiency versus public information—reaches into such elementary aspects of museum management as the labelling of exhibits. Much labelling is simply an extension of the museum scholar's expertise. If a Chinese collection is labelled "Ming Dynasty," and the visitor knows nothing about Ming, he will simply have to suffer his own ignorance. There are even cases in which museums provide no labelling but a kind of ceremonial naming presumed to be self-evident to the viewers. At the Louvre the Venus of Milo and the Victory of Samothrace are identified as being, in fact, that: the Venus of Milo and the Victory of Samothrace. They are treated, in other words, not so much as works of art or even specimens of Greek civilization, but as archeological and aesthetic "celebrities" or self-explanatory monuments of "our culture," whose significance and importance any respectably cultivated person is expected to know.

The problems created by excessively scholarly or insufficiently informative labelling are, then, intimidation and cultural shame in the first case, confusion in the second. Understandably, therefore, it has become the practice among the more enterprising museums to aid the visitor with free brochures which, through some combination of showmanship, casualness and taste, attempt to make him less solemn about scholarship and more confident of his own sensitivity, thus inducing what one curator calls "guilt-free" museum going.

There remains one other contradiction between the museum as a communal institution and the "inherent" nature of the artifacts which it houses. As an educational institution it should be the museum's principal mission to make available—to diffuse, as the French say—a visible semblance and example of higher cultural creativity, and to awaken in the public a sense of understanding and respect for it. To do this they do not actually have to have in their possession great works of art. Reproductions, as art history courses testify, should be enough. But museums, as we know, are what the sociologist Hans Zetterberg calls "beauty banks," repositories of literal treasures and physical monuments.

They have also been called temples, a metaphor which comes remarkably close to fact. Most of the great museums in the United States and Great Britain and many in continental Europe are built in the Greco-Roman style which signals the presence of a civic sanctuary; in this, as in the untouchability of the objects and the hushed decorum demanded of the visitors, there is much that is symbolically and behaviorally religious in nature.

The focus of this religion is, of course, the work of art conceived as a sacred object, whose sacredness emanates from two things: the holiness of art itself, and the object's originality in the material sense—its quality, that is, of being physically "an original," a special creation, a singular production, not a reproduction, a replica or a copy. The significance of the *original* may be related to nineteenth century romantic notions of the radical uniqueness of creativity (which made the artist god-like in his powers, a force bringing "all" out of "nothing"). But it may also be related to the ritual connotations ("the first born," the "only begotten") of such Western traditions as primogeniture. In any case, neither art museums nor the art market could exist or be understood without "originals," their aura, and their sumptuously priced rarity (a "priceless" work of art is usually one of enormous monetary value).

The possession of originals is, of course, decisive for the public ranking of art museums, and for the social uses to which those possessions are put. From the point

of view of their civic prestige, the great storehouses of
art are the great storehouses of art *originals*. And local
as well as regional institutions which could perform a
much greater service to the art education of their
communities by the wide use of reproductions, not only
do not do this, but rather compete for whatever
originals they may be able to acquire, even when their
artistic merit is doubtful.

Furthermore, the great reverence for originals mili-
tates against some of the specific didactic tasks of art
collections. It is the rule in great museums that they
never defile their most valued original possessions by
using them as illustrations of artistic or historical
development. Paintings by Rubens or Greco are intrinsic
entities: "a Rubens," "a Greco." Separate masters stand
separately, sometimes in rooms of their own. Art
treatises or textbooks may show a Franz Hals next to a
Vermeer to make a point of difference in style within a
national tradition. But the Rijks Museum in Amsterdam
does not. Just as the Prado does not hang portraits by
Velázquez, Greco and Goya in sequence as episodes in
the history of Spanish painting. Even the French
Impressionist Museum (the *Jeu de Paume),* one of
whose rooms is dedicated to examples of the fine detail
of the style and the stages of its development, uses for
this purpose *photographs* of canvasses which hang
elsewhere in the building. "Within the walls" museums
still regard the didactic as secular and the contemplative
as sacred. Education may be the task of a gallery lecture
or "talk," but great works of art must not themselves be
pressed into such service.

The art museum is, then, a "medium," and today
unquestionably a "mass medium." It is also an educational one. To say the latter, however, presupposes that

museums already know what they wish to communicate, what can be communicated and to whom. But my impression is that the nature and the basis of the symbolic relationship between art museums and their public is not yet known, and that the relationship which is now imagined to exist may turn out to be, in some cases, neither a dream nor a reality for the public.

Like most museums, art museums are often ancestral places, the ground on which the present meets the past in the most self-conscious and organized fashion. But the past is the past, regardless of how democratically we may make it available to the present. Cobbett might still ask today, as he did in 1833, how things created for the amusement of the privileged can be regarded as the rightful spiritual possession of the ordinary man. For the fact is, of course, that in spite of all the rhetorical utterances about "our heritage," in most cases that heritage is not really ours. When the present-day museum visitor, perhaps the child of a working class family, perhaps the descendant of an eighteenth century yeoman, encounters Van Dyck's portrait of Charles I, with its air of indolent, inaccessible self-assurance and subtle mortification at the common world, does he look upon it as art, as history, as curiosity, as a vague manifestation of grandeur, as an object of awe and obeisance, of anger, *moral* suspicion, class antagonism or amused incomprehension?

Museum officials worry a great deal these days about what they call the archaic orientation of some of the great art repositories of the Western world. What they mean by this is, in part, the secret or open preference of museum staffs for the ideal of the elite visitor. However, the deeper questions of the art museum's role and place in modern society may not be answered until we know

the manner in which the present appropriates the past.
Until, in fact, we know the perception—cultural, historical and social—which the visitor has of the museum and
of his own relationship to it.

April 1967

Authority in the Comics

ARTHUR A. BERGER

In the last few years there has been what might be called a "comic craze." It started with the discovery that Batman was "camp." Batman's enormous success on television spread to the stage with Superman and led to such things as Jules Feiffer's anthology of "classic episodes" called *The Great Comic Book Heroes*. If the comics are " . . . a basic expression of American culture [and a] reflection of the predominant values in the life of the United States," as social psychologist William Albig put it in *Modern Public Opinion,* then perhaps we should take a better look at them than we have done in the past.

Because comic strips are popular in other countries, they furnish a very useful means for comparing attitudes and values. I recently made a study of some representative American and Italian comics (*fumetti* in Italian) and

217

discovered that they reveal profoundly different attitudes toward the subject of authority.

For example, let us examine how the "military" is
treated in American and Italian comics. The differences
are so striking as to suggest that there are fundamental
differences between the two cultures in general.

The great Italian "antimilitary" comic hero is Marmittone (1928) by Bruno Angoletta. Like many of the
earlier Italian comics, it is very simply drawn with rather
stiff, wooden figures, plain backgrounds and dialogue in
the form of rhymed verse (which appears in captions
underneath the drawings). As in most comics, the
dialogue isn't really necessary; it only adds details,
although the rhyme and humor of the poetry are very
amusing to children.

Marmittone is an extremely enthusiastic and zealous
soldier who, as a result of bungling or bad luck, always
ends up behind bars. Most of his adventures involve
accidentally discomfiting officers or their friends and
being reprimanded by being sent to the guardhouse.
Marmittone is not rebellious at all. Indeed, he is just the
opposite—he respects authority figures. He exhibits no
desire to "cross" them, and if it were not for the fact
that he is "jinxed" or perhaps even "doomed," he
would be a model soldier. The only thing negative in the
comic strip is that the hero, for whom we have affection
and sympathy, ends up in prison—a dark, empty room
into which a symbolic ray of light is always seen filtering.
It thus seems that something must be wrong if Marmittone, a good-willed hero, can end up in jail. But no direct
attack is made on the officers; they are only obliquely
ridiculed, and always at the expense of the hero.

In American "antimilitary" comics such as Mort
Walker's Beetle Bailey the attack is more direct. In this

strip, currently one of the most popular in America, the common soldier consistently engages in the battle of wits with his superiors and generally emerges victorious. The sergeant and the captain in Beetle Bailey are both relatively sympathetic antagonists whose cupidity and stupidity endear them to the reader. It is the enlisted men who have the "upper hand" most of the time because they have the brains and because authority is not seen as valid. The sergeant is a good-natured, boisterous glutton and the lieutenant is foolish and childish.

What's more, the ridicule is pictorial. In one episode, for example, the sergeant is seen coming through the "chow" line. He has a tray loaded with steaks, potatoes, salad, etc. "Wait," he says to the mess sergeant, "I don't have any celery." He also doesn't have any ice cream but the mess sergeant tells him there is no room on his tray and adds that there is "no coming through the line twice." The dilemma is solved by stuffing celery in the sergeant's ears and ice cream in his mouth. He thus "succeeds" but at the price of becoming a clown.

A contemporary Italian military strip dealing with the adventures of Gibernetta and Gedeone is somewhat closei to Beetle Bailey, though it retains the humorous poetry captions of Marmittone, and still has a reverential and respectful attitude toward authority. Rather than ending in prison as Marmittone always does, Gibernetta and Gedeone generally are awarded medals. The "fall guy" or the victim is the sergeant who blunders and suffers for it. Since receiving a medal is seen as a proper reward for the heroes, then the officers, the real authority figures, are still seen as *legitimate*. The sergeant, who is only instrumental in executing the wishes of the officers is also, we must remember, an enlisted man who has risen—but he is still not a true authority figure.

Possibly the artist who draws the strip, Cimpiani, was influenced by Walker, for his hero, Gibernetta, at times looks strikingly like Beetle. He has the same round head, his hair sticks out wildly from under his cap, his legs are thin and like toothpicks (this applies to all Cimpiani's characters); the only real difference is that you can see Gibernetta's eyes, whereas Beetle's are usually hidden under his cap.

Few of the "classic" Italian comics (such as Bonaventura, Bilbolbul, Pier Cloruro, or Pampurio) have the highly stylized, toothpick limbs and big feet that you find in Disney characters, such as Mickey Mouse. Both this kind of stylization and exaggeration and the realistic, "draftsman" type *fumetti* (which aren't usually comic) are more or less American innovations, and fairly recent ones at that. Mickey Mouse dates from 1928 and "draftsman" style *fumetti* from Milton Caniff's Terry and the Pirates, 1934.

Mickey Mouse, known as Topolino in Italy, is probably the most important comic strip figure in Italy. He is the hero of at least one weekly magazine, *Topolino,* and a monthly one, *Almanac of Topolino.* Both magazines contain Donald Duck and other Disney characters and have some adventures that are written specifically for the Italian public. Almost 30 percent of the readers are between 16 and 34 years of age, which suggests that a good many of the fathers of children reading Topolino also read it. (The weekly edition has a circulation of 260,000 copies and *Almanacco* has a circulation of 140,000 copies per month.)

The Disney characters have a "supra-national" appeal because they are simple animals and indulge in slapstick-filled cops-and-robber chases and activities amusing to all children. Donald Duck, Mickey Mouse and their friends have also inspired a host of imitators so that there is now a comical cartoon character for almost every animal that exists.

But why should a mouse be so popular with children? Possibly because the mouse is a small, defenseless and "household" creature that most children have seen, with whom they can empathize, and of whom they need not be afraid.

Historically, Mickey Mouse is a descendant of the mouse Ignatz in one of the greatest American comics, Krazy Kat, which flourished between 1911 and 1944 (until Herriman, its creator, died). But Krazy Kat was very different from Mickey Mouse. Ignatz Mouse was a decidedly antisocial character constantly in rebellion against society, whereas Mickey Mouse is well adjusted, internalizes the values of his society, and is on the side of "law and order." He is comforting to children since he shows that submitting oneself to the values of a given order ends in well-being, rewards and acceptance.

In the older "classics" of Italian and American comic repertoires, we find another interesting pair of "antisocial" animals, the American mule, Maud (1906), and the Italian goat, Barbacucco (1909).

Both animals are pitted against human beings—the goat butts people and the mule kicks them, but there is an important difference in the consequences. While Maud always ends up "victorious," the goat's actions always come to nothing. For example, he will butt a tree in which a boy and a girl are sitting and the fruit will fall down, which they then eat. On the other hand, all attempts to "tame" Maud, the ornery mule, are useless and people who try are most always defeated, though they might have momentary and temporary successes.

Maud is a rebel who succeeds; Barbacucco is a rebel who does not, and perhaps, in a strange way, they mirror two different attitudes: the American type of self-sufficient individualism and the Italian idea that somehow the "given order of society" is too strong to be bucked, that things are "fated." Whether the fates are smiling or not is beside the point, for if things are ultimately fated, individual initiative and efforts are of no great importance—"whatever will be will be."

Probably the best example of this reliance "on the gods" is the famous Italian comic hero, Bonaventura, who started amusing children in 1917. Graphically, Bonaventura is typically "old school" Italian—the figures are stiff and crudely drawn, little attention is paid to landscape (which is highly stylized and greatly oversimplified), there is not much expression on the faces of the characters, there is much fantasy, and the dialogue is given in rhymed verse captions.

Things do not *always* turn out well for Bonaventura (which means "good adventures" or "good luck"). When he instigates actions and activities—such as trying to drive a car or trying to become a social lion—things turn out badly for him and he generally retreats and goes back to simpler ways and more secure activities. It is only by chance (even the malicious acts of his nemeses are chance events) that potential "disasters" turn out well for him, and he earns his *milione* (fortune). Thus, at the end of an episode in which Bonaventura tries to drive automobiles, with calamitous results, he decides that from now on he will walk; or at the end of an adventure in which he tries to "enter society," he decides that society is full of delusions and that he will remain with his sweet and good family. For reasons such as these, I think we can call Bonaventura a decidedly *conservative* character, or one who embodies a conservative outlook toward experience.

This, in turn, suggests that Bonaventura isn't as optimistic a strip as is commonly believed in Italy. Bonaventura's "rebellions" against the more cloying aspects of family life or the limitations of being a pedestrian end in defeat. And even when he gets his *milione* it is generally the result of a freak occurrence, it is always rather "miraculous." Individual initiative is played down and luck is all; the best of all possible rewards is seen as money. Bonaventura is a materialist who emphasizes for readers that the only way to become a success in the world is through a miracle—not a particularly hopeful outlook.

There are several other comparisons between American and Italian comics that suggest differences in attitudes toward royalty and aristocracies and the treatment of the "mischievous" child.

Soglow's "The Little King," which started appearing in 1934, is very close to the classical Italian comic in style, but far different in attitude. The king, a fat dwarf who has a big mustache, always wears his crown and generally an ermine robe. But he is humanized. He fetches the milk in the morning, he rushes to bargain clearances in department stores, and is generally shown to be "just like anyone else." He is made into a good democrat, and there is no suggestion of any divinity "that doth hedge a king." Indeed, both the title of the strip, "The Little King" and the fact that he is mute, indicate this.

Rubino's "Lola and Lalla" is much different. Here, Lola, the daughter of a rich man (we have an aristocracy of wealth here), is always elaborately dressed and quite vicious toward Lalla, her social inferior. Lalla is always shown in "modest but clean" clothing, decidedly inferior to that of Lola. As a result of being pushed around by Lola, however, she ends up with more beautiful clothing. Generally this is accomplished by having some sticky substance fall on Lalla to which flower blossoms become attached.

Here the aristocracy, as represented by Lola, is seen as vicious and brutal, repulsing any attempt by the common people (Lalla) to be friendly or to gain recognition. Social class is shown by clothing, as in "The Little King." But whereas the king is warm and very human, as we might expect from a democratic American king, the European aristocracy is demonic and insists that the people "know their place." Social mobility is impossible and any attempts at it are repulsed. Even Lola's dog, conventionally a friendly animal, is shown as nasty and cold, corrupted, we imagine, by his relationship with Lola and the "upper classes."

A similar attitude in Italian comics deals with "naughty" children. That is, in many of the episodes the mischievous child is caught and punished; the price of rebellion is a spanking or some kind of humiliation. This is different from many American comics, in which the child often succeeds.

Take, for example, Rubino's remarkable strips Pierino and Quadratino, which appeared from 1909 on. Pierino is a little boy who is always trying to get rid of his doll, but never succeeds. He buries it, he gives it away, he throws it down the chimney—but no matter, it keeps coming back. Generally in the last panel the same shaft of light that fell on Marmittone in jail now falls on Pierino, although in this case the ray of light probably symbolizes internalized conscience rather than socially "objectionable" activities.

Quadratino is a boy whose head is a cube. His escapades generally result in his head getting changed in shape, so that the fact that he has committed "crimes" becomes visible. There is much distortion in the strip and a good deal of plane geometry. But the moral of Quadratino (and of Pierino) is that bad boys always get caught or, in more general terms, rebellion against properly constituted authority is perilous and futile.

It might be objected that Hans and Fritz, the Katzenjammer Kids also usually end up being punished, and this is true. But there is an important difference to be noted between the endings in the Katzenjammer Kids and in Rubino's strips. Generally, the pranks of Hans and Fritz are successful and cause a great deal of discomfort to the adults against whom they are directed. Thus, the pranks are successful as pranks. It is only the fact that adults, having a monopoly on force, can get their revenge—and do so—that pales the victories of the kids (and tans their hides).

Let me summarize the underlying psychological and social attitudes in these comics and which I am hypothesizing might be broadly accepted cultural values:

ITALIAN COMICS

Character	Attitude to Authority
Marmittone (1928-1953)	respects constituted authority, zealous, but jinxed
Gibernetta (contemporary)	respects authority
Barbacucco (1910-1924)	unsuccessful in his rebellion against people

Bonaventura (1917-1965)	bad luck turns out miraculously for the best, conservative approach to experience
Lola and Lalla (1910-1913)	interaction between classes impossible, upper classes seen as demonic
Quadratino (1910) and Pierino (1909)	rebellion against authority (adult world) seen as futile

AMERICAN COMICS

Character	Attitude to Authority
Beetle Bailey (1953-present)	authority not recognized as valid
Mickey Mouse (1928-present)	values of the given order are valid
Ignatz Mouse (1913-44)	anti-social and rebellious
Maud (1906)	anti-social and rebellious (successfully)
Little King (1934-present)	democratic "King"—no different from anyone else
Katzenjammer Kids (1898-present)	rebellion against adult world successful in short run, but often has bad consequences

These Italian comics reflect a basically conservative approach toward experience and society. Authority is generally portrayed as valid and rebellion against it as futile. Social mobility must depend on miracles in a rigid and hierarchical society in which all attempts to climb are brusquely repulsed.

The American comics described here suggested, on the other hand, an irreverential approach toward authority. Authority is often invalid, and not necessarily worthy of respect. So there is much more antisocial and rebellious activity, which is seen as possibly successful. Mickey Mouse is the only conformist of the group; but then Mickey, as I have already pointed out, is also very popular in Italy.

These conclusions are, of course, tentative—they have been drawn from a rather limited reading of a rather small group of comics. On the other hand, these comics cover a wide range in time and concept, and some of them can rightly be considered to be classics. Moreover, I did not choose them because they dealt with authority, but merely tried to compare comics that were similar in time and subject (for instance, Maud and Barbacucco). I found that with a number of important strip characters the outstanding difference revolved around the way authority was treated.

It is, I think, much more than coincidence that these values found in the comic strips parallel closely what social scientists and skilled observers have had to say for a long time about the different attitudes toward authority in the United States and other countries. For example, De Tocqueville said in *Democracy in America:*

To the European, a public officer represents a superior force: to an American, he represents a right. In America, then, it may be said that no one renders obedience to man, but to justice and law. If the opinion which the citizen entertains of himself is exaggerated, it is at least salutory; he unhesitatingly

confides in his own powers, which appear to him to
be all-sufficient.

Recently, Glen H. Elder Jr. studied family authoritarian-
ism in five countries and found that Italy was the most
authoritarian country and America the least authoritarian one. This would suggest, then, that comics
accurately reflect values and are worthy of more serious
attention.

December 1966

Notes on Contributors

Ralph L. Andreano ("The Affluent Baseball Player") is director of the Health Economics Research Center, department of economics, University of Wisconsin. He is the author of numerous books and journal articles, and is continuing his research on the economic impact of disease and health.

Michael Armer ("Athletes Are Not Inferior Students") is an associate professor of sociology at Indiana University. Armer is engaged in research on the social and psychological effects of formal education in non-industrial societies.

Joseph Bensman ("Classical Music and the Status Game") is professor of sociology at City College and on the Graduate Faculty of the City University of New York. His most recent book is *The New American Society* (with Arthur J. Vidich). He is the author of books, articles and essays on the sociology of the arts.

Arthur Asa Berger ("Authority and the Comics") is an associate professor in the Social Science Department at San Francisco State College. Berger has published articles in this area in America and Italy. He is now working on projects in advertising and drug abuse and is writing a book on the comics as social history.

George Gmelch ("Magic in Professional Baseball") is a doctoral candidate in the department of anthropology of the University of California at Santa Barbara. Formerly a professional baseball player, Gmelch is now studying sports sociology and culture change. He has worked in Mexico and Ireland, and his dissertation topic is the adaptation of Irish Tinkers (itinerants) to settled life.

César Graña ("The Private Lives of Public Museums") is the author of *Modernity and its Discontents* and the forthcoming *Fact and Symbol: Essays in the Sociology of Art and Literature.* He is currently professor of sociology at the University of California at Santa Cruz.

Robert LaFranchi ("Why People Play Poker") is a law student at the University of San Francisco.

Janet Lever ("Soccer as a Brazilian Way of Life") is in the department of sociology, Yale University. She is studying children's toys, and plans to return to Brazil for a further look at soccer and its effects. She is co-author of *Women at Yale: Liberating a College Campus.*

Helena Znaniecki Lopata ("The Dance Studio—Style Without Sex") is professor and chairman of the department of sociology at Loyola University of Chicago. *Occupation: Housewife* is her latest book and *Widowhood in an American City* is in preparation.

E. Louis Mahigel ("Making *vs.* Playing Games of Cards") is a doctoral candidate in communication and teacher in the Department of Speech, Communication and Theater Arts at the University of Minnesota. His interests include interpersonal and organizational communication.

Thomas M. Martinez ("Why People Play Poker") is an assistant professor of sociology at Stanford University. Martinez is continuing his studies on gambling and is also doing research on the psychological consequences of ethnic stereotyping in the mass media.

Joseph R. Noel ("The Dance Studio—Style Without Sex") is an assistant professor of psychology at the University of Chicago. He has written or edited numerous publications, most currently a book entitled *I-We-Thou: Dimensions of Being.*

Richard A. Peterson ("Audiences and All that Jazz") is an industrial sociologist and professor of sociology and anthropology at Vanderbilt University. Peterson is interested in the music industry and has written articles and books on social problems and change.

Ned Polsky ("Of Poolrooms and Pool Playing") teaches sociology at the State University of New York at Stony Brook. He is the author of *Hustlers, Beats and Others,* and is presently compiling a chronology of the humanities in Western civilization, *Annals of the Arts & Humane Learning.*

Gregory P. Stone ("Making *vs.* Playing Games of Cards") is a professor of sociology at the University of Minnesota. He has contributed many articles on play, sport and non-verbal communication and has co-edited *Social Psychology Through Symbolic Interaction. (For more detail, see the cover.)*